The Politics of Democratic Representation

This book discusses boundaries of electoral inclusion and mechanisms of electoral representation in contemporary democracies.

While the ancient Athenians took the idea of rule by the people to require direct popular participation in public decision-making and the appointment of officials by lottery mechanisms, democracy is nowadays interpreted electorally. We partake in government mostly by electing the legislative, and sometimes executive, officials who in turn make the substantive decisions. Yet, who "we" is and how electoral representation should function remains hotly contested. Controversies abound about the proper configuration of the demos – the body of persons who are enfranchised – and the ways it is to exercise electoral choice and agency. This book takes up several carefully selected questions from these theoretical and political debates. Looking at the (dis)enfranchisement of children, cognitively disabled persons and refugees and discussing the forms of representation that might be afforded to external voters, future generations and non-citizens, the contributions develop innovative arguments applying the basic principles of electoral democracy to the complexities of specific, real-world cases. Doing so, the contributions offer timely, yet unorthodox, perspectives on the theory and practice of electoral democracy.

This book was originally published as a special issue of *Critical Review of International Social and Political Philosophy.*

Benjamin Boudou is Professor of Political Theory at the University of Rennes, France.

Marcus Carlsen Häggrot is a political theorist and post-doctoral researcher at Sciences Po, France.

The Politics of Democratic Representation

Enfranchisement and Participation Revisited

Edited by
Benjamin Boudou and Marcus Carlsen Häggrot

Routledge
Taylor & Francis Group
LONDON AND NEW YORK

First published 2025
by Routledge
4 Park Square, Milton Park, Abingdon, Oxon, OX14 4RN

and by Routledge
605 Third Avenue, New York, NY 10158

Routledge is an imprint of the Taylor & Francis Group, an informa business

British Library Cataloguing-in-Publication Data
A catalogue record for this book is available from the British Library

ISBN13: 978-1-041-04320-1 (hbk)
ISBN13: 978-1-041-04323-2 (pbk)
ISBN13: 978-1-003-62781-4 (ebk)

DOI: 10.4324/9781003627814

Typeset in Myriad Pro
by codeMantra

Publisher's Note
The publisher accepts responsibility for any inconsistencies that may have arisen during the conversion of this book from journal articles to book chapters, namely the inclusion of journal terminology.

Contents

Citation Information

The following chapters in this book were originally published in *Critical Review of International Social and Political Philosophy*, volume 26, issue 5 (2023). When citing this material, please use the original page numbering for each article, as follows:

Introduction

Electoral representation revisited
Benjamin Boudou and Marcus Carlsen Häggrot
Critical Review of International Social and Political Philosophy, volume 26, issue 5 (2023), pp. 629–634

Chapter 1

Is child disenfranchisement justified?
Nico Brando
Critical Review of International Social and Political Philosophy, volume 26, issue 5 (2023), pp. 635–657

Chapter 2

Universal enfranchisement for citizens with cognitive disabilities – A moral-status argument
Regina Schidel
Critical Review of International Social and Political Philosophy, volume 26, issue 5 (2023), pp. 658–679

Chapter 3

Should refugees in the European Union have voting rights?
Ali Emre Benli
Critical Review of International Social and Political Philosophy, volume 26, issue 5 (2023), pp. 680–701

Chapter 4

Legislative expatriate representation: A conditional defence of overseas constituencies
Marcus Carlsen Häggrot
Critical Review of International Social and Political Philosophy, volume 26, issue 5 (2023), pp. 702–724

Chapter 5

What's wrong with the presentist bias? On the threat of intergenerational domination
Anja Karnein
Critical Review of International Social and Political Philosophy, volume 26, issue 5 (2023), pp. 725–746

Chapter 6

Representing non-citizens: A proposal for the inclusion of all affected interests
Benjamin Boudou
Critical Review of International Social and Political Philosophy, volume 26, issue 5 (2023), pp. 747–768

Notes on Contributors

Ali Emre Benli's research focuses on the ethics of immigration, democratic theory and theories of civil disobedience. He is the co-editor of *Claiming Citizenship Rights in Europe*. His work has been published in the *Journal of Global Ethics* and the *Journal of Refugee Studies*.

Benjamin Boudou is Professor of Political Theory at the University of Rennes, France.

Nico Brando is Newton International Fellow at Queen's University Belfast and the University of Liverpool, UK. He does research in Political and Moral Philosophy, working on issues of discrimination in human rights and children's rights.

Marcus Carlsen Häggrot is a political theorist and post-doctoral researcher at Sciences Po, France.

Anja Karnein is Associate Professor of Philosophy at Binghamton University (SUNY), USA. She works broadly on issues surrounding social justice, including its domestic, global and intergenerational implications, as well as on questions of deontological morality more generally.

Regina Schidel is a post-doctoral researcher at Goethe University Frankfurt, Germany. Her research interests include disability in political theory, theories of human dignity and human rights and moral and social philosophy.

Introduction: Electoral Representation Revisited

Benjamin Boudou and Marcus Carlsen Häggrot

Electoral representation is a cornerstone of contemporary democracy. Democracy today is widely interpreted to mean that the people governs itself through electing officials of government. But while this notion of democracy through electoral representation is firmly entrenched, its constitution in practice is hotly contested.

One point of contention is notably how a democracy should define its 'demos', i.e. the body of persons who are enfranchised and entitled to exercise electoral agency. Democratic theorists notoriously disagree whether the demos should include all persons who (in some sense) will be affected by the demos' decisions (e.g. Bengtson, 2021; Fung, 2013; Goodin, 2007), or whether the demos should include only the persons who will be legally subjected to the demos' decisions (e.g. Beckman, 2008; Honohan, 2018; Owen, 2012). Additionally, there are disagreements, too, about the enfranchisement of certain groups. For instance, it is debated whether or not the franchise should be extended to youth aged less than 18 years (e.g. Beckman, 2009; Lau, 2012; López-Guerra, 2014; Umbers, 2020), and analogous controversies exist with respect to resident non-citizens (e.g. Goppel, 2021; López-Guerra, 2014; Owen, 2010), non-resident, expatriate citizens, (Bauböck, 2007; Lopez-Guerra, 2005; Rubio-Marin, 2006) and convicted criminals (e.g. Cholbi, 2002; Poama & Theuns, 2019), too.

In addition to these disagreements about the proper remit of the demos, theorists of democracy and the general public also disagree on the shape of electoral structures and rules. It is a long-standing controversy, for example, whether single-member-district elections are a justifiable system for electing legislators or whether proportional electoral systems are distinctively preferable (e.g. Christiano, 1996; McGann & Van der Hout, 2009; Wilson, 2019). Equally, there is an intricate debate on whether electoral structures should include mechanisms such as electoral quotas, reserved legislative seats, and group-conscious districting practices to guarantee representation to certain disadvantaged groups, especially women, ethnic and indigenous minorities, and the working class (e.g. Cagé, 2020; Mansbridge, 1999; Phillips, 1998; Williams, 1998).

Finally, there is disagreement as well on the potential limits of electoral representation and the tools that might appropriately remedy them. For instance, one current debate weighs whether electoral procedures ought to be complemented with non-electoral representation mechanisms such as deliberative mini-publics or randomly selected legislative chambers (e.g. Abizadeh, 2021; Fishkin, 2011; Lafont, 2019; Landa & Pevnick, 2021). Equally, theorists discuss the modes of political participation and inclusion that a democratic polity should afford to beings unable of exercising electoral agency, e.g. animals or future generations.

The constitution of electoral representation is thus intensely controversial, with debates covering an immense variety of issues. In this special issue, the contributors consider a number of carefully selected questions that have emerged from these debates. Looking at the (dis)enfranchisement of children, cognitively disabled persons, and refugees, and discussing the forms of representation that might be afforded to external voters, future generations, and non-citizens, the contributions develop innovative arguments that unite the analysis of the basic principles of electoral democracy with a rigorous scrutiny of the complexities of specific, real-world cases. Doing so, the contributions offer timely yet unorthodox perspectives on the theory and practice of electoral democracy.

The first three contributions by Nico Brando, Regina Schidel, and Ali Emre Benli each engage in the debate about the proper definition of the demos. Brando specifically looks at the case of children, developing a comprehensive, critical analysis of the arguments that are standardly advanced to justify their political disenfranchisement. Brando argues that child disenfranchisement cannot be compellingly justified on the grounds of unawareness or because disenfranchisement protects particular goods of childhood. Defences that hone in on children's political incompetence fare better. However, Brando argues, they are only available to those endorsing an epistemic conception of democracy and do not, in any case, justify the selective disenfranchisement of children only.

Schidel, for her part, considers the case of citizens with severe cognitive disabilities, who are also commonly disenfranchised. Schidel contends that this disenfranchisement reflects an ableist bias and neglects the unique, valuable contributions that these citizens can make to politics. She further argues that enfranchisement is central to the constitution of relational equality. Therefore, cognitively disabled citizens should be enfranchised and allowed to benefit from assisted voting, i.e. voting by a proxy who votes according to expressed will of the disabled person. However, Schidel rejects the more radical practice of substitutive voting, where proxies vote according to their assessment of the disabled person's will and interest, as this carries risks of abuse and does not necessarily further relational equality.

Last in this series, Benli studies the case of refugees in the European Union. Taking as axiomatic the all-subjected principle of democratic inclusion, Benli argues that refugees are subjected both to member state policies and to policies decided by EU bodies, and that refugees therefore in principle should be enfranchised both for national-level elections and for EU parliament elections. For the national-level enfranchisement, though, Benli argues that it should occur only after a period of residence to sufficient to ensure the development of democratically important skills and dispositions, notably linguistic skills and a sense of trust and solidarity with the host society. For the EU parliamentary elections, by contrast, Benli argues that the requisites of these skills and dispositions are less stringent, and that refugee enfranchisement there ought to be immediate.

Following these analyses of particular groups' claims to enfranchisement, Marcus Carlsen Häggrot's contribution addresses a question of electoral structure. Focusing on the case of expatriates voting in home-country elections, Carlsen Häggrot asks whether in a constituency-based electoral system, such voters should be included into existing, in-country constituencies, or whether they should be grouped into special overseas constituencies. Rejecting existing treatments of the question as unsatisfactory, Carlsen Häggrot proposes to answer it by analysing the competing models in terms of their democratic qualities. Carlsen Häggrot shows that when expatriate voters form a small part of the overall demos, overseas constituencies are better able to sustain equality of political influence, different forms of deliberation, and practices of partisan voter mobilisation, and thus he concludes that special overseas constituencies are sometimes the more desirable form of expatriate representation.

Finally, in the last two contributions, Anja Karnein and Benjamin Boudou discuss the limits and possible extensions of electoral democracy. Karnein concentrates on the case of future generation, arguing that democratic decision-making in the present can be dominating for future generation. Certain present-day decisions, Karnein argues, create such existential threats for future generations that they must continuously and comprehensively devout their energies to solving those threats. If such purpose-determining decisions are taken presently without sufficient consideration for future generations' interests, a form of domination is present. Karnein further contends that such domination is objectionable, and she correspondingly advocates that present-day democratic decision-making be re-structured to guard against the neglect of future generations' interests. Specifically, Karnein proposes that future generations might be represented by a dedicated body specifically in the domains where purpose-determining decisions are possible, and that there might be a justiciable right for future generations to self-determination to enable present citizens to contest political decisions in the name of future generations.

Boudou, on the other hand, focuses on the case of non-citizens living abroad and asks specifically what the inclusion of their affected interests implies for their case. Taking for granted that a demos has to be bounded, Boudou argues that the globalisation of a democracy's demos is not a viable route to achieve the all-affected principle of democratic inclusion. However, he does not conclude that the principle is unsound. Rather, Boudou shows that the interests and viewpoints of non-citizens can be represented effectively in a democracy through a variety of non-electoral representation mechanisms, such as reciprocal representation arrangements amongst different national legislatures, through ombudsmen, or advocacy groups. At the same time, Boudou notes that these mechanisms have a number of weaknesses that require attention, which leads him to conclude that the representation of non-citizens constitutes a second-best but realistic route to satisfy the demands of the all-affected principle.

Disclosure statement

No potential conflict of interest was reported by the author(s).

ORCID

Benjamin Boudou http://orcid.org/0000-0003-2309-7303
Marcus Carlsen Häggrot http://orcid.org/0000-0003-2476-0453

References

Abizadeh, A. (2021). Representation, bicameralism, political equality, and sortition: Reconstituting the second chamber as a randomly selected assembly. *Perspectives on Politics, 19*(3), 791–806. https://doi.org/10.1017/S1537592719004626

Bauböck, R. (2007). Stakeholder citizenship and transnational political participation: A normative evaluation of external voting. *Fordham Law Review, 75*(5), 2393–2448. https://ir.lawnet.fordham.edu/flr/vol75/iss5/4

Beckman, L. (2008). Democratic inclusion, law, and causes. *Ratio Juris, 21*(3), 348–364. https://doi.org/10.1111/j.1467-9337.2008.00394.x

Beckman, L. (2009). *The frontiers of democracy: The right to vote and its limits*. Palgrave Macmillan.

Bengtson, A. (2021). Where democracy should be: On the site (s) of the all-subjected principle. *Res Publica*. 28, 69–84 . https://doi.org/10.1007/s11158-021-09511-6

Cagé, J. (2020). *The price of democracy: How money shapes politics and what to do about it*. Harvard University Press.

Cholbi, M. (2002). A felon's right to vote. *Law and Philosophy, 21*(4/5), 543–565. doi:10.2307/3505059.

Christiano, T. (1996). *The rule of the many: Fundamental issues in democratic theory*. Westview Press.

Fishkin, J. S. (2011). *When the people speak: Deliberative democracy and public consultation*. Oxford University Press.

Fung, A. (2013). The principle of affected interests: An interpretation and defense. In J. H. Nagel & R. M. Smith (Eds.), *Representation: Elections and beyond* (pp. 236–268). University of Pennsylvania Press.

Goodin, R. E. (2007). Enfranchising all affected interests, and its alternatives. *Philosophy & Public Affairs, 35*(1), 40–68. https://doi.org/10.1111/j.1088-4963.2007.00098.x

Goppel, A. (2021). Prior residence and immigrant voting rights. *Moral Philosophy and Politics*. https://doi.org/10.1515/mopp-2020-0004

Honohan, I. (2018). Republicanism and the all subjected principle as the basis of democratic membership. In R. Bauöck (Ed.), *Democratic inclusion* (pp. 143–159). Manchester University Press.

Lafont, C. (2019). *Democracy without shortcuts: A participatory conception of deliberative democracy*. Oxford University Press.

Landa, D., & Pevnick, R. (2021). Is random selection a cure for the ills of electoral representation? *Journal of Political Philosophy, 29*(1), 46–72. https://doi.org/10.1111/jopp.12219

Lau, J. C. (2012). Two arguments for child enfranchisement. *Political Studies, 60*(4), 860–876. https://doi.org/10.1111/j.1467-9248.2011.00940.x

Lopez-Guerra, C. (2005). Should expatriates vote? *Journal of Political Philosophy, 13*(2), 216–234. https://doi.org/10.1111/j.1467-9760.2005.00221.x

López-Guerra, C. (2014). *Democracy and disenfranchisement: The morality of electoral exclusions*. Oxford University Press.

Mansbridge, J. (1999). Should blacks represent blacks and women represent women? A contingent "yes". *The Journal of Politics, 61*(3), 628–657. https://doi.org/10.2307/2647821

McGann, A., & Van der Hout, E. (2009). Proportional representation within the limits of liberalism alone. *British Journal of Political Science, 39*(4), 735–754. https://doi.org/10.1017/S0007123409000684

Owen, D. (2010). Resident aliens, non-resident citizens and voting rights. In G. Calder, C. Phillip, & J. Seglow (Eds.), *Citizenship acquisition and national belonging: Migration, membership and the liberal democratic state* (pp. 52–73). Palgrave Macmillan.

Owen, D. (2012). Constituting the polity, constituting the demos: On the place of the all affected interests principle in democratic theory and in resolving the democratic boundary problem. *Ethics & Global Politics*, *5*(3), 129–152. https://doi.org/10.3402/egp.v5i3.18617

Phillips, A. (1998). *The politics of presence*. Oxford University Press.

Poama, A., & Theuns, T. (2019). Making offenders vote: Democratic expressivism and compulsory criminal voting. *American Political Science Review*, *113*(3), 796–809. https://doi.org/10.1017/S0003055419000297

Rubio-Marin, R. (2006). Transnational politics and the democratic nation-state: Normative challenges of expatriate voting and nationality retention of emigrants. *New York University Law Review*, *81*(1), 117–147. https://ssrn.com/abstract=3134064

Umbers, L. (2020). Enfranchising the Youth. *Critical Review of International Social and Political Philosophy*, *23*(6), 732–755. https://doi.org/10.1080/13698230.2018.1511172

Williams, M. (1998). *Voice, trust, and memory: Marginalized groups and the failings of liberal representation*. Princeton University Press.

Wilson, J. L. (2019). *Democratic equality*. Princeton University Press.

OPEN ACCESS

Is child disenfranchisement justified?

Nico Brando

ABSTRACT

Children are among the few social groups that are systematically and universally disenfranchised. Although children are citizens worthy of equal moral treatment and rights, their right to vote is restricted in almost all states, and this is seen as legitimate by most democratic theories. What is particular about childhood that justifies the restriction of their right to vote? How can democratic systems legitimise the exclusion of a section of their citizenry? This article provides a critical analysis of the principles that ground child disenfranchisement, and of the allocative mechanisms proposed for restricting the right to vote. It shows that most arguments in favour of child disenfranchisement are unsatisfactory, as they are inconsistently used to target the child population (but not other groups) or are incompatible with a commitment to equality. Among the principles for child disenfranchisement, only those that appeal to political incompetence may be valid for excluding children. Regarding the allocative method of exclusion, this article shows that age thresholds cannot be justified to restrict franchise, and that, while competence tests fare better in theory, there may be issues of implementation. The article contributes by providing a clear and systematic analysis of the core arguments in favour of child disenfranchisement, and the conditions that must be met to justify such a practice.

Introduction

Children are among the few citizen groups that are systematically and universally disenfranchised.[1] While in recent decades various countries have lowered their voting age to 16, this is an exception to the rule that being a minor means not having the right to vote.[2] This article explores the main arguments used to support the systematic disenfranchisement of children. It aims to show that most principles used to justify disenfranchisement are invalid, and that neither age thresholds, nor competence tests, are fully satisfactory as methods for exclusion.

Two elements are at play in justifying disenfranchisement: a claim about *the principle for disenfranchisement*, and a claim about *the appropriate method to select a section of the population to disenfranchise*. This article looks at these two elements separately, and critically analyses how the philosophical literature attempts to justify child disenfranchisement both in terms of principle and selection method. It, thus, answers to the justifiability of child disenfranchisement by breaking it into two separate issues:

1. *Principle for Disenfranchisement*: What are the legitimate reasons for restricting the right to vote to a citizen?[3]

2. *Method of Disenfranchisement*: What mechanisms are available to legitimately select which citizens can be justifiably disenfranchised and which cannot?

While it may seem that the justifiability of child disenfranchisement is a binary affair (either it is justified or it is not), the subject is much more complex. The literature appeals, sometimes implicitly, to one of three *principles* to justify disenfranchisement of children: *the unawareness principle* considers that children are not affected by not having voting rights as they are unaware of what they are missing, so their equal standing is not harmed by disenfranchise; *the best interest principle* argues that it does not benefit children to bear political rights and responsibilities, as it imposes unjust burdens on them; finally, *the harm to democracy principle* argues that child enfranchisement threatens the legitimacy of a democratic system, due to children's political incompetence. This article claims that only arguments that appeal to harm can provide legitimate reasons for disenfranchisement. However, it argues that the justifiability of the harm principle depends on how the legitimacy of democracy is understood: if democratic legitimacy relies on ensuring *political equality among its citizens*, then child disenfranchisement cannot be justified; if democratic legitimacy relies on ensuring *quality procedures and outcomes*, then disenfranchisement can be justified.

Standing on 'harm to democracy' as the only principle that can potentially justify child disenfranchisement, the article looks at the three main methods proposed to exclude from franchise: age-thresholds as proxy for political incompetence, substantive competence tests, and procedural competence tests. It argues that age-based categorisations cannot be justified, especially if they are the sole indicator used to track incompetence. As to competence tests, in principle, both substantive and procedural tests are more legitimate mechanisms for allocating franchise (as they do not discriminate children based on age); however, their justifiability is affected by whether one gives more value to the equality or quality dimensions of democracy. If democracy is valued predominantly due to its epistemic capacity to produce quality outcomes, competence tests can be justified. But if democracy is valued predominantly due to its egalitarian credentials, competence testing cannot be used as a method for allocating franchise.

The article contributes to the literature by providing a clear and systematic analysis of the core arguments in favour of child disenfranchisement, and the conditions that must be met to justify such a practice. It claims that disenfranchisement is justified only if the legitimacy of democracy is threatened by political incompetence. However, age cannot be used as an indicator for tracking political incompetence; if political incompetence is of concern, it ought to be tracked for everyone regardless of age. Restricting the right to vote based on age is patently discriminatory, and should be abolished.

Section 2 analyses three principles used to justify disenfranchisement of children (unawareness, best interests, and harm to democracy). Section 3 assesses the validity of three mechanisms for exclusion from franchise (age thresholds, substantive competence testing, and procedural competence testing). Section 4 concludes.

Principles for disenfranchisement

To assess the justifiability of child disenfranchisement, we must begin by analysing the validity of the reasons given to restrict the right to vote to children. If democratic processes aim to recognise some form of equal standing among citizens, how can the exclusion of some citizens from franchise be justified?

Unawareness and self-respect

A first argument in favour of child disenfranchisement claims that children are not democratic equals as they are not affected by (or unaware of) being excluded from the political process. One could read Thomas Christiano's (2001) argument in favour of child disenfranchisement as relying partially on this justification.[4] Christiano claims that, beyond political incompetence (see Section 2.3), children are justifiably excluded from the democratic process as 'their status is not undermined by exclusion from collective decision making about matters pertaining to justice' (Christiano, 2001, p. 207): children are unaffected by exclusion as they lack awareness of the 'facts of judgment' (*Ibid.*).

López-Guerra (2012) follows a similar line of argument, while focusing on the individual's interest in self-respect. He claims that enfranchisement has a distributive and a relational value. Unequal distribution of voting rights affects individuals' interests because it, first, provides unequal opportunities to affect decision making; and, second, because they harm the self-respect of those who are not granted equal political rights (López-Guerra, 2012, p. 126). While all citizens would be unjustly treated due to the distributive inequality of disenfranchisement, not everyone is unjustly treated based on voting's relational value. Children under 10-years-old, he argues, even if harmed in distributive terms, are not misrecognised by disenfranchisement as their self-respect is not affected by not being allowed to vote (López-Guerra, 2012, p. 127).

Christiano and López-Guerra thus claim that individuals whose self-respect (or lack of awareness of the facts of judgment) is not affected by disenfranchisement may be justly disenfranchised. This misses an important element of the problem of respect: unawareness of being disrespected does not preclude disrespect. Both authors assume that the harm caused by lack of inclusion is conditioned by the subject's awareness of her mistreatment and the harm it causes. This is far from true. Relying on an individual's own awareness of their disrespect for it to be considered an injustice has problematic implications, particularly for the protection of the vulnerable and dependent. Take, as an example, laws that protect children from sexualisation through prohibitions of child pornography or sexual exploitation. These protections are especially stringent precisely because most children who are sexually exploited are unaware of the objectification and harm caused by being treated as sexual objects. It is their lack of awareness of being treated sexually what makes their sexualisation so problematic. If one appealed to unawareness as justifying disrespect in this case, the whole system that protects children (or individuals with mental disabilities) from sexual exploitation would be lost, especially in the most terrifying cases, as younger children are less aware of the harm that is inflicted on them through disrespect. I believe that appealing to unaffectedness as the principle that justifies disenfranchisement is unsatisfactory, and can have grave consequences on the interpretation of other cases in which lack of awareness to harm is present.

Philip Cook's proposal for a minimum procedural competence test (2013) can be considered as a partial endorsement of the unawareness justification for disenfranchisement, while not relying (entirely) on the argument presented above. Cook argues that disenfranchisement can be justified by defining a minimal procedure through which the individual must pass in order to vote (tracking literacy and independence; Cook, 2013, pp. 450–455). The procedure limits enfranchisement only to those aware of it, while filtering out those who would be unaffected by being disenfranchised: 'As those incapable of completing these tests would be ignorant of the test, they would not suffer harm to self-esteem' (Cook, 2013, p. 454). Cook proposes a radical change in the threshold for inclusion, expanding enfranchisement to almost all the population, while still justifying disenfranchisement for those whose illiteracy or dependence makes them unaffected by (or unaware of) their exclusion.

While Cook's is one of the most consistent and fair proposals in the literature, I still wish to raise an issue with his justification for disenfranchising those who do not pass a procedural test: namely, its irrelevance. If the procedural test aims at excluding those, and only those, who are entirely unaware of their exclusion, it seems that the test is unnecessary as it filters out individuals who would most probably not be a part of the procedure anyways. What would change if they were enfranchised, and simply did not vote? Within Cook's own understanding of the competences required for enfranchisement, recognising the right to vote to those unaware and unaffected by disenfranchisement (who would be a very small fraction of the population) would not have an impact on the democratic outcome whatsoever (Hinze, 2019, p. 297), while it would play an important symbolic role in recognising all citizens as equal members in society.

The question of principle, thus, cannot be answered by appealing to children's unawareness and unaffectedness of being excluded from franchise. First, assuming unawareness of harm as legitimising disrespect is highly problematic; second, the unawareness claim (if true) would only apply to a minority of the child population, making disenfranchisement irrelevant.

The best interests principle

An alternative argument claims that franchise harms children's fundamental interests (Beckman, 2009, 2018). The principled justification is that enfranchisement would harm children's best interests. The concept of 'best interests' grounds Beckman's claim that children's interests may be harmed by enfranchisement. He argues that children's political rights ought to be determined primarily with reference to their best interests (Beckman, 2009, p. 92). Following the Convention on the Rights of the Child (CRC; UN General Assembly (UNGA), 1989, Art. 3.1), children's best interests must be the primary concern when making any decision that may affect them. Thus, whether children ought to have voting rights should rely on an assessment of the benefits and harms that this may incur. Due to children's vulnerabilities and developmental needs, primary concern should be given to understanding the (positive and negative) impact that voting has on their fundamental interests (Beckman, 2009, p. 114; see also, Clayton, 2006, p. 183).

Relying on the 'best interests' principle, Beckman follows the literature on the 'special goods of childhood' (C.M. Macleod, 2010; Gheaus, 2015) to argue that granting political freedoms to children, with the duties this entails, threatens the protection and promotion of a core interest that children have *in being children*. Beckman uses the moral wrongness of child labour as an analogy: 'The reason why children have no moral right to take employment is not that children are particularly bad workers but that to work is bad for them.' (Beckman, 2018, p. 291). It is not that children are necessarily incapable of voting; rather, the claim is that certain goods specific to 'being a child' (i.e. freedom to play, freedom from political burdens, and innocence from adult affairs) would be compromised by their enfranchisement. Voting would impose responsibilities on children, limiting the realizability of the goods of childhood: children would bear the burden of making decisions over society as a whole, they would be compelled to use their free time to acquire information and knowledge on political options and on deliberation over their decisions (Beckman, 2009, p. 115; see also, Schrag, 2004, p. 373). It is, thus, claimed that it is not in children's best interest to engage with political questions and bear political responsibilities; their best interests justify their disenfranchisement.

There are three problems with this line of argumentation: one lies in its interpretation of the 'best interests' principle, the second is empirical, and the third substantial. First, Beckman's interpretation of the support that the CRC's 'best interests' principle gives to his argument is flawed.[5] Part of the reason why the 'best interests' principle exists is for it to partially compensate for children's lack of political rights (Eekelaar & Tobin, 2019). The 'best interests' principle requires accounting children's own views and claims in order to decide what is best for them. This means that children's interests cannot be conceptualised unidirectionally by external actors, as Beckman presumes; within the CRC, children must be included in the deliberation over what these interests are, and how to realise them (Eekelaar, 1994; UN General Assembly (UNGA), 1989 Art. 12).

The 'best interests' principle is not a pre-emptive justification for unilaterally deciding what is best for all children (Eekelaar, 1994); it is a dynamic principle that should adapt to the particular circumstances of particular children, balancing the reasoning of experts *with children's own views on what their own interests are* (Skivenes, 2010). It is not mean to be used as a ground for generalisable prescriptions for the whole childhood population; but rather to accommodate what justice requires to individual circumstances. Claiming, as Beckman does, that the best interests of all children would be necessarily harmed by enfranchisement obviates both children's own views on the subject, and the variable impact that franchise can have on children in different stages of development (Archard & Skivenes, 2009).

One could avoid the above issue by not appealing to the CRC, and state that the argument relies on a paternalistic definition of children's best interests (Beckman, 2009, p. 114). It would, however, still fall prey to an empirical and a substantive critique. As to the empirical issue, Beckman unduly inflates the burdens and responsibilities that come with voting to make his point. He claims that children's interests in free time and play would be irremediably harmed due to the responsibilities of being enfranchised (Beckman, 2009, p. 115). This is not necessarily the case. If we assumed that every voting citizen has the duty to acquire all necessary information and to deliberate in a fully reasonable and rational way, then, not only would children not have any free time left, but possibly everyone else would have to spend all their time deliberating politically. No one expects the individual citizen to bear the burden of democracy to this extent (López-Guerra, 2012, p. 130). Imposing this requirement on children when the rest of the population does not comply with it would be patently unjust. An even if it were so, the fact that children are enrolled in schools can palliate the threat of this responsibility taking over their free time and play (Umbers, 2020, p. 738). One could conceive of civic education classes during school time (which is already not free nor time for play) targeted particularly to children's acquisition of political information, and as a forum for debate on the different positions and candidates on the ballot (Franklin, 2020; Mahéo & Bélager, 2020).

Even if children's interests in free time and play are not affected, a 'best interests' argument could claim that political innocence, and an interest in being shielded from the 'adult world' could be threatened by enfranchisement. As Rehfeld rhetorically asks: 'Do we want, for example, a 12-year-old to deliberate about how best to deal with female circumcision in Africa or debate whether waterboarding is a good or bad policy of interrogation?' (Rehfeld, 2011, p. 153). The claim is that children have a fundamental interest in being innocent; in being shielded from certain realities that political rights uncover (C. Macleod, 2015).

This line of argument is problematic for more substantial reasons than the former. Appealing to innocence to justify the restriction of fundamental rights begs various questions: can 'innocence' be defended as an objective and universal value that justifies such restriction? Shouldn't children themselves have a say in what constitutes their interest in innocence? Using the political discourse of 'innocence' to restrict a group's rights has bad pedigree. Jane Rutherford (1997, pp. 1479–1489), for example, showed how the discourse of 'protecting innocence' was used against the suffragette movement during the turn of the twentieth century. Although it could be argued that the case of children is different from that of women (children are in fact innocent, while women are not), there are still problems in applying it to this case (Jenks, 2005, Ch. 6).[6]

As Joanne Lau argues, '[c]alling someone 'innocent' is often a covert form of oppression; it is a failure to take him or her seriously as a political agent.' (Lau, 2012, p. 861). Innocence implies a refusal of having to justify to those we deem as 'innocent' why we keep them in this state; while, at the same time, not providing any actual content to what 'innocence' entails, or why it is beneficial to be innocent. The concept proposes a highly moralised conception of what 'childhood' should be, assumes it as true (and objectively good), and then imposes it unilaterally. Each of these steps would require thorough justification for the argument to hold. First, one must justify the imposition of a WEIRD[7] conception of 'childhood' without accounting for the variability of who children are (Lancy, 2015, pp. 397–399). Children are a radically heterogenous group (depending on their age, where they live, and other intersections); thus, claiming that innocence from the adult political world is good for them (in general) fails to account for this plurality of the childhood experience, and how engaging with reality may benefit or harm them (Jarkovská & Lamb, 2018, p. 78). Second, one must show why political innocence is necessarily good for the child population. Many children do not have the option of 'being shielded from the adult world': they are caretakers, workers, heads of households; they are treated differently because of their gender, race or religion; they care about climate change, social justice, war. Many children live already (for better or worse) in the adult world, and disenfranchising them will not change this situation, nor make them innocent again. I do not see how disenfranchisement can be justified based on children's best interests when children are forced to live in adult worlds, or when they value being political.

An argument for disenfranchisement that relies on the 'goods of childhood', and on a paternalistic understanding of children's best interests does not stand. It does not account for children's own voice and agency in defining what their best interests are; it overestimates the harms that may be imposed on children by voting; and it assumes that interference is justified regardless of the particular condition of different children.

Harm to democracy, and political incompetence

If the act of voting affects the legitimacy that the democratic process is meant to secure, then it might be justified to withhold franchise from those who can harm the system. Most (if not all) democratic theorists agree, at least in principle, that harm to the legitimacy of the democratic system can justify disenfranchisement. As voting gives political power to the individual, it allows voters to wield coercive authority over others (Brennan, 2011). Certain voters can vote 'wrongly', and if collectively the majority vote 'wrongly', this would threaten the legitimacy of democracy.

The 'wrongness' of voting can be interpreted in two ways: as generating 'bad' outcomes, or as being construed in the 'wrong' way (Estlund, 2008, pp. 160–167). While some democratic theorists directly mention bad outcomes as a potential problem with the democratic system (i.e. Caplan, 2006; Estlund, 2008; Goodin and Lau 2011), most agree that the threat to the legitimacy of the system lies in citizens voting through corrupt cognitive processes (i.e. ignorance, bias, irrationality, unreasonableness). The assumption is that, if the individual's cognitive process of deliberation is flawed, the system is corrupt, and the results are illegitimate (Brennan, 2016).[8] In short, voting wrongly can either lead to bad political outcomes that harm others, or it makes the system lack legitimate authority to rule.

Some form of harm can justify limiting the political power of individuals. If a democratic system cannot protect its citizens from the worst public bads, or if it systematically elects the worst possible candidates and the worst possible policies, what is the use of having a democratic system (besides its symbolic value) (see, Brennan, 2016: Ch.1)? Harm to democracy, thus, seems to be a justified principle for disenfranchisement, and one can see how children may fit into this picture: if it can be shown that children vote 'wrongly', their disenfranchisement might be justified.

A just cause, however, is insufficient to disenfranchise a particular collective. Justifying disenfranchisement requires showing that the morally relevant traits track the outcome one wants to avoid. In this case, *political incompetence* is considered the most relevant trait that traces an individual's proneness to cause harm to democracy through voting.[9] Choices made through the democratic process have an ample impact on everyone in society, and, so the argument goes, those who are allowed to vote should be *competent enough* to do so.

Individuals who are less competent in doing X are more likely to cause harm to others while doing X than individuals who are more competent (Christiano, 2001, p. 197). Less competent voters are more likely to harm through their votes than more competent voters, thus, a distribution of political power that tracks incompetence is justified to ensure that democratic decisions are made only by those competent to do so (Brennan, 2011, p. 709). Political powers and privileges are conditioned and limited by the harm they may inflict on others. If one does not have the competence required to ensure that one's actions do not cause relevant harms, it is legitimate to have one's actions restricted. In the case of children, the capacities required for being politically competent come with maturity, thus, it may be legitimate to disenfranchise the youngest population as they are those with highest probability to cause harm through their low political competence.

What does it mean to be 'politically competent'? A politically competent person is characterised, not by the content of their political choices, but by the process through which they make these political choices. As Christiano argues, political competence 'is a disposition of a person. It does not entail always having the right answer. One may be morally competent but make mistakes or have the wrong moral views ... or act irresponsibly.' (Christiano, 2001, p. 200). It is not necessarily about choosing the 'correct' option on a ballot; it is about choosing through the 'correct' cognitive process. It entails reaching a certain level of rationality and reasonableness, which allows one to form and revise one's conception of justice and the good, and to understand and abide by fair terms of cooperation (Fowler, 2014, pp. 99–100). It entails a minimal ability to understand what the democratic process is, and one's responsibility in being part of this process (Archard, 2004, p. 101; Chan & Clayton, 2006, pp. 538–542).

The acceptance of political incompetence as justificatory of disenfranchisement assumes the epistemic reliability of the democratic system: democracy has value because it can produce correct political outcomes more reliably than alternative political systems. This assumption is based on Condorcet's 'jury theorem': if a voter's has fifty-one percent or higher probability of choosing correctly among a set of options, then the system can be expected to produce correct outcomes reliably (Goodin & Lau, 2011). For this to be achieved, however, it must be ensured that the average voter's probability of making a correct choice is better than a fifty-fifty chance (see, Estlund, 2008, Ch. 8, esp. 156–158); this requires ensuring that the majority of the electorate is not politically incompetent (with fifty-fifty or less probability of making a correct choice). Children, it is argued, due to their low political competence, would lower the quality of democratic choices to be worse than fifty-fifty, thus, must be excluded, as the epistemic reliability of the democratic system requires it (Chan & Clayton, 2006).

One can respond in one of two ways to this claim: first, by showing that the quality of the democratic process would not be harmed by including the politically incompetent; or second, by appeal to the egalitarian value of democracy, claiming that the outcome is secondary if in tension with the principle that all should be recognised as equals in the democratic process.

Many defenders of the enfranchisement of the 'incompetent' have argued, based on Condorcet's 'jury theorem,' that the inclusion of children and other 'incompetent' collectives would not have a negative impact on the quality of the democratic process as the probability of the average voter choosing incorrectly is inexistent (Goodin & Lau, 2011; Munn, 2018). If the quality of the process is of concern, then individual political competence is irrelevant; only the collective competence of the whole electorate (understood as average competence) can allow us to assess whether the outcome would be reliable (Hinze, 2019). Children's votes would not reduce sufficiently the average individual competence to affect the outcome; children's votes would be, at worst, random, thus simply increasing the number of votes without affecting the outcome (Goodin & Lau, 2011, p. 160), or, due to the influence of competent voters (such as their parents, teachers, etc.), their political choices would reflect those of informed voters, thus, actually improving the overall quality of the outcome (Olsson, 2008).

The Condorcetian response is appealing as it shows that, if most voters are sufficiently apt at choosing a correct option, it is irrelevant whether the rest are competent or not. The response, however, has limitations: first, it requires average competence of the collective to be sufficiently adequate for it to withstand incompetent voters; and, second, its focus on the quality of the outcome does not answer to the claim of legitimate authority.[10]

Regarding the first point, conceding to the correctness of the jury theorem, if average individual competence has a fifty-fifty chance, or worse, of making correct choices, then the system cannot withstand more incompetent voters

(Brennan, 2016: Ch. 2). As the Condorcetian argument relies on the assumption that the average competence of the electorate is in fact sufficiently adept in making correct choices, its validity depends on this empirical assumption being true: if the average voter votes badly in a systematic way (due to incompetence or moral corruptness) then the system cannot withstand the inclusion of a larger, potentially incompetent electorate. Moreover, it would actually require increasing the threshold of competence (or moral righteousness), disenfranchising many more, to ensure average individual competence to be better than random.

Going further, Jason Brennan (2011) argues that whether the outcome is correct or not is irrelevant to justifiability, as political incompetence makes the *procedure* illegitimate. Competence is fundamental to voting, not only because it improves the chance of better outcomes, but because *the legitimate authority of the process depends on it.* Brennan (2011, pp. 702–705) uses the legitimacy of jury decisions as an example that proves the moral relevance of competence. He asks whether a jury that we know as ignorant of the facts of the case, or one which is incapable of understanding what the case is about and what its consequences are, can be considered as a legitimate authority (Brennan, 2011, p. 708). He claims that, regardless of what the outcome is (that is, whether the jury's decision is right or wrong systematically), the jury must be considered as illegitimate as no system of justice should rely on individuals who are incompetent making these high stakes choices. Brennan claims that the case of voting is analogous to juries; only those deemed capable of voting rationally, consciously and knowledgably should be allowed to do so; the authority and legitimacy of the system depends on this.

Brennan's legitimacy-based argument is strong. However, the validity of this claim presupposes that democracy merely has an instrumental value in ensuring quality political outcomes (Brennan, 2016, pp. 10–14). Democracy, for more proceduralist theorists, is valuable because it is a political system that recognises and reflects the equality of its members beyond its instrumentality (i.e. Christiano, 2002; Kolodny, 2014). In this sense, the right to vote 'is a symbolic affirmation of one's political status even when it seems to have little instrumental value for an individual.' (Archard, 2004, p. 98). Seeing democracy through this lens would imply that the quality of the outcome should be secondary to the egalitarian condition that democracy stands on. Legitimate democratic authority, a proceduralist would claim, does not arise from quality outcomes, but from the recognition by the process of the equality of all citizens *regardless of competence* (Goodin, 2007).

One can agree that the egalitarian rationale of the procedure has fundamental value, while defending the need to account for the instrumentalist challenge. Would a proceduralist abide by a democratic process so incompetent (or morally corrupt) that would undermine the principles upon which it stands? Conceding to the egalitarian procedural value of democracy, the threat to the legitimacy of the system by an excess of political incompetence or moral corruptness must be taken as a limit to what the procedure can withstand. Some minimal conditions that safeguard the legitimacy of the democratic system from widespread incompetence or corruptness must be in place to secure its stability.

What does this entail? The weight one assigns to different values of democracy determines to a great extent the scope of justifiability of disenfranchising based on political incompetence. Does democracy *reflect* the equality of those citizens who meet the competence for being treated as equals (as instrumentalists argue)? Or does democracy *recognise and symbolise* the equal political status of all citizens regardless of an individual's condition (as proceduralists maintain)?[11] For the task at hand, it suffices to say that, on the one hand, understanding democracy as mainly instrumental can justify more stringent requirements for inclusion to the franchise; on the other, valuing democracy primarily for its egalitarian procedures, while it shrinks the justified scope of disenfranchisement based on incompetence, it still must concede to ensuring that the legitimacy of the system is protected from systematic corruptness or incompetence. Whether procedural or instrumental, widespread political incompetence is a threat that no democratic system can withstand; disenfranchisement that prevents this scenario is, thus, justified.

Method of disenfranchisement

Following the previous section, only threats to the legitimacy of the democratic system through political incompetence can justify restricting franchise for children. Having determined the principle that could ground disenfranchisement, we must explore the justifiability of the mechanisms available for classifying who may be included or excluded from franchise based on incompetence.

Age as a threshold

Age is the standard metric used to track political incompetence and enforce child disenfranchisement. If you are below a certain age (usually 18-years-old) , you are deemed legally incompetent to exercise the right to vote. But why can age be used to justify disenfranchisement? Age is not morally relevant in itself; it is useful only as a proxy that tracks political (in)competence. Competence variability between a 17 and an 18-year-old is so subtle (if it even exists) that it would be arbitrary to judge every 18-year-old individual as competent and every 17-year-old as incompetent. The cognitive and emotional development that occurs with age is so fluid and variant from person to person, that using any particular point as a definite and accurate threshold seems highly questionable (Fowler, 2014, p. 100; Cook, 2013, pp. - 444–445).

What justifies, then, treating individuals above and below an age threshold differently? Two arguments are given. First, the justifiability of statistical discrimination: even if age is not an accurate distinguishing trait, the statistical probability that individuals at each side of the threshold will behave as expected (underaged as politically incompetent, adults as competent), proves the proxy as reliable even if not precise (see, Schauer, 2018). Second, one can appeal to complete-life egalitarianism to respond to concerns that age proxies are discriminatory: a commitment to equality does not entail treating individuals equally at each moment in their life; equality only requires individuals being treated equally across their whole lifespan. If everyone's voting rights are restricted below a certain age, complete-life equality is secured.

Using age as the threshold for disenfranchisement relies on the existence of a relevant correlation between age and the development of the competences deemed necessary for voting (Archard, 2004, p. 89). Even if unprecise tracking political incompetence, it is satisfactory as it is easy to implement, transparent, and sufficiently reliable if one considers the difference in competence between individuals of a very young age and middle-aged adults (Hinze, 2019, p. 292). Defenders of an age threshold, such as Archard (2004, Ch. 6), argue that even if there is contention regarding the accuracy of age at the boundaries of the threshold (the difference between a 17 and an 18-year-old are insignificant), the progressive acquisition of competences, and clear difference in competence of the cases at the extremes proves the justifiability of the threshold. The validity of speed limits while driving works as an analogy: we need speed limits because of the risk of accidents when speeding; despite that risk does not vary if driving at 99 or 100 km/h, the difference between driving at 100 or 30 km/h proves the justifiability of a threshold, even if not precise (Archard, 2004, pp. 86–89). Same with voting: the obvious incompetence of a one-year-old justifies the establishment of a threshold even if not fully accurate at the boundaries; 'What matters is the overall balance of probabilities. We need only to be confident that the competence is most probably not possessed by those in one age group and most probably possessed by those in the other.' (Archard, 2004, p. 89).

Age thresholds do not count as instances of wrongful discrimination because they rely on statistical correlation to justify its differential treatment (Clayton, 2006, p. 186). Opposed to discrimination based on gender or race, which are triggered by biases or prejudices against a collective, discrimination based on age uses statistical correlation of age and political competence to determine its threshold (Chan & Clayton, 2006, p. 539). The method is not unjust because it accurately tracks the probability of incompetence collectively, even if it does not individually. Results of a statistical study by Chan and Clayton (2006) exploring political competence of individuals at different ages shows a correlation between willingness to participate in political activities, ability and knowledge on politics and democracy and age. Thus, they argue, current age limitations on voting are justified.[12]

The argument for statistical discrimination has problems, particularly in how it applies to age-based disenfranchisement: first, statistical data, even if accurate, can be self-fulfilling and spurious; second, even if not discriminatory in itself, it may be discriminatory if applied exclusively to the under-18 age group.

Statistical discrimination is particularly problematic as it may suffer from circularity and self-fulfilment by relying on information taken from a system that discriminates in order to assess whether the discrimination is justified (Lister, 2007; Lau, 2012, p. 863). An important reason why minors are statistically less competent and interested in politics is not because of their inherent lack of capacities, but rather due to the absence of incentives provided for them to develop these capacities (see, Peto, 2018). Imagine if Chan and Clayton's (2006) survey of political competence had been used to assess the political interest and knowledge of men and women prior to female enfranchisement in the early-nineteenth century. Most surely the results would show that the female population had a radically lower interest in and capacity to understand and address political questions than the male population. But this is not an objective assessment; it does not prove women's counterfactual political incompetence; it seems self-fulfilling as it merely shows that, under conditions in which it was close to impossible for women to acquire political competence, women did not possess said competences.

Proving the current political incompetence of children under restrictive conditions is insufficient to justify their disenfranchisement. These types of surveys show that we need to improve the conditions that would allow children to become politically competent (Peto, 2018, p. 282). If individuals have the potential to become competent, they should have ensured the conditions needed to develop this ability (Brando, 2020). Empirical research on political competence shows that an outstanding difference exists between the competence of enfranchised and disenfranchised minors; comparison between political competence of adolescents in Austria (where 16-year-olds are enfranchised) and the UK (who are disenfranchised) shows that enfranchisement makes a difference in how competent minors are (i.e. Mahéo & Bélager, 2020; Wagner et al., 2012). What this means is that without the existence of a counterfactual scenario in which we can assess political competence without restrictive background conditions, the claim of statistical reliability is spurious, and, thus, questionable as justification for disenfranchisement (Mahéo & Bélager, 2020, p. 5, 18; Peto, 2018, pp. 290–292).

A second problem with the current use of statistical discrimination is its inconsistent application to different age-groups (or to other indicators relevant to political competence). Even if statistical discrimination were justified, the fact that it is used exclusively to restrict the rights of one collective can be unjust (Hinze, 2019, p. 295). Assuming that age-based statistical discrimination is valid, Joanne Lau (2012) has argued that it can only be implemented if it applies symmetrically to the elder population at the other end of the age spectrum as well. She claims that if age is relevant, it should be used as an indicator of incompetence at all stages of life, not only childhood (Lau, 2012, pp. 864–865). The only justified way to use age as a proxy for incompetence is by tracking its correlation across the whole lifespan and disenfranchise age groups according to their statistical incompetence (Fowler, 2014 proposes a similar system). This revision of the statistical discrimination argument, while not fully successful addressing the issue of using age as an indicator, at least overcomes one of the issues that affect disenfranchisement based on age: the fact it only applies to the youngest age-groups.[13]

Following complete-lives egalitarian theory (Daniels, 1988), some defenders of age thresholds for disenfranchisement (Clayton, 2006; Fowler, 2014; Weale, 1999) argue that differential treatment based on age is justified, opposed to discrimination based on gender or race, because age discrimination affects everyone equally. '[D]iscrimination on the grounds of age is fundamentally different from discrimination because of gender or race. Since everybody ages, policies that appear to be unfair to elder or younger groups might in fact be justifiable when looked at over the whole lives of the individuals concerned.' (Fowler, 2014, p. 104ff). We all pass through the same stages of life in which our voting rights are restricted, and this restriction lasts the same for everyone; it does not violate equality and may be considered as justified allocative criteria for differential treatment. If what matters is whether individuals are treated equally across their complete lives, the restriction of certain rights (such as voting) based on age does not violate the ideal of equality, and is, therefore, justified (Clayton, 2006, pp. 188–189).

Appealing to complete-lives egalitarianism may be sufficient to show how allocation of rights based on age complies with equality while other forms of differential treatment do not, but it fails to provide sufficient justification as a method of disenfranchisement as it does not offer an argument in favour of any particular allocation of voting rights (Umbers, 2020, pp. 746–747). The complete-life egalitarian argument is insufficient to legitimise that the present age-based system in which only children are disenfranchised is the appropriate mechanism to abide by equality. Because it focuses exclusively on ensuring equal treatment across the life-span, many allocative mechanisms besides the current would comply with its tenant: imagine a system in which one has five years of enfranchisement then five years of disenfranchisement, or another in which only the elderly are disenfranchised, or another in which random ages are chosen to disenfranchise (López-Guerra, 2012, p. 125; Lau, 2012, p. 868). From a complete-life egalitarian perspective, there is no difference in choosing one or another; its minimal focus on the protection of equality across life does not suffice to justify specific allocative methods, nor to prove why it should only track children.

Even if age works as a simple, easily enforceable, and clear allocative mechanism for disenfranchisement, its lack of accuracy, and its reliance on dubious statistical information makes it a morally problematic method for tracking political incompetence.

Testing competence

Theorists who maintain that political incompetence justifies disenfranchisement, but doubt the validity of age proxies, have explored competence-testing as an alternative threshold for exclusion. The arguments against age proxies looked exclusively at how children are discriminated or harmed by their age-based disenfranchisement. However, the problem with using age as a proxy for political incompetence goes beyond its negative impact on the disenfranchised population; it also bestows an unfair privilege to the politically incompetent who are not tracked by age (Munn, 2018). If political incompetence is the morally relevant trait that justifies disenfranchisement, then the metric used to track political incompetence ought to track it *always*, not just some instances of it. Even assuming that all individuals below the age of 18 are indeed politically incompetent and, thus, justly disenfranchised, as a matter of consistency we still ought to track and disenfranchise those above the age of 18 who are politically incompetent (Lau, 2012; Munn, 2018). If political incompetence threatens democracy, then every politically incompetent citizen should be disenfranchised.

Just as it is credible to argue that some (or most) children are indeed politically incompetent, it would not be ridiculous to claim that there is a threatening section of the enfranchised population who by any account of political competence would qualify as incompetent, thus, a threat to democracy. If failure to abide by public reason and the 'facts of judgment' is an instance of political incompetence (Christiano, 2002); if ignorance of basic facts about politics, candidates and issues is an instance of political incompetence; if proneness to manipulation, bias, and an incapacity to make independent political choices is an instance of political incompetence, then, as Brennan argues, not only should many (or all) children be disenfranchised, but a majority of the adult population should be disenfranchised also (Brennan, 2016; see also, Caplan, 2006).

What these competences are, what their threshold should be, and how they should be assessed, however, are contentious issues. One can divide, for simplicity, between defenders of substantive and procedural competence tests (Christiano, 2001; Cook, 2013). Endorsers of substantive tests of competence consider that people's political competence must be evaluated through testing knowledge about the facts of the political and the electoral systems, assessing biases in reasoning, the capacity to understand the issues, and the consequences of political choices (Brennan, 2011; Munn, 2012). Substantive tests impose a high threshold to enfranchisement by ensuring that only fully reasonable and rational individuals can vote.

Procedural tests, on the other hand, filter incompetence out of the suffrage while keeping the threshold low enough for democracy's commitment to equality to not be affected. Instead of demanding 'ideal' political competence from its citizens, procedural tests filter through transparent and uncontroversial means whether a citizen is competent to vote. Cook, for example, proposes a purely procedural test in which the act of registering to vote and voting independently are themselves the procedure that determines whether an individual is politically competent (in this minimal sense; Cook, 2013, pp. 450–454). The procedural test assesses literacy through an individual's act of registering to vote, and assesses independence through an individual's act of voting privately in a booth. These are, for Cook, sufficient and minimal requirements for voting; nothing else should be expected from an individual to justify their enfranchisement.

A couple of problems have been raised with competence tests. First, the question might be raised as to whether tests should track the ideal competence for democratic politics, or if they should track the minimum requirements that could be expected from the citizenry (Archard, 2004, p. 101–102; Fowler, 2014, pp. 96–97). It is claimed that appealing to the first, ideal, understanding of what a citizen should know about politics, and how she should reason about politics, asks too much from the general population. If democracy is valued both for its instrumental reliability *and* for its egalitarian distribution of political power, a substantive test with a high threshold would threaten its egalitarian credentials, leading to an epistocratic system which few true democrats would be willing to endorse (see, Umbers, 2020, p. 742). If political equality is a valued tenet of democracy, imposing such high requirements for the franchise would be inconsistent with its core commitments.

While the above critique hints at procedural tests as better suited than substantial ones as an allocative method for franchise, a second issue affects both substantive and procedural tests: they may be biased against certain populations, incentivising abuse and discrimination (Archard, 2004, pp. 90–91). Biased tests demanding literacy were used in the past to exclude black Americans from U.S. elections (Rutherford, 1997; Cook, 2013, p. 442). Even today, voter ID laws, and voter registration procedures can be biased against social groups, affecting effective enfranchisement (Braconnier et al., 2017; Hajnal et al., 2017). Although such policies are not necessarily crafted with discriminatory intentions, they can end up being discriminatory as there is a high chance that the competences required to pass the test are more prominent in people with higher education, and higher socioeconomic status, thus excluding whole socioeconomic classes, or sections of the population (Estlund, 2008, p. 217–218; Umbers, 2020, p. 749). Brennan (2011, p. 720) has responded to these claims by arguing that this is not an injustice caused by the tests themselves, but rather that the tests reflect an already existing injustice: lack of access to education and political resources for certain sections of the population. In theory, ensuring a fair distribution of educational and political resources would compensate this potential injustice.[14]

These discourses bring to the fore an important tension, and a potential inconsistency, at the root of mainstream democratic theory: democracy's attempt, first, to strike a balance between its procedural and instrumental values, and, second, to be consistent and fair in the way it does so, means that there may be important conceptual trade-offs that are not straightforward, and which tend to be omitted when discussing the case of child enfranchisement (Hinze, 2019). On one side, if the instrumental value of democracy is considered as sufficiently important to trump equality, then political competence must be taken seriously as a trait that has to be tracked and tested, to ensure the sustainment of a reliable and legitimate democratic system. If, however, the egalitarian procedures of democracy are considered its most fundamental quality, then democracy must be willing to give up a certain level of instrumental reliability, and attempt to lower the threshold of expected competence in order to enfranchise most (if not every) citizen.

Concluding remarks

This article explored the main arguments that attempt to justify the disenfranchisement of children. It considered three principles for disenfranchisement (unawareness, best interests, and harm to democracy), and argued that only arguments that appeal to harm to the democratic system based on political incompetence can justify the restriction of franchise. Based on this, it studied two methods used to select which groups count as 'harming democracy' (age thresholds, and competence tests). It claimed that age thresholds are unacceptable for disenfranchising, and considered the credentials of substantive and procedural competence tests in assessing political incompetence. Neither test is fully justifiable, and most of their validity depends on how the value of democracy is understood. Instrumentalist approaches to democracy are more amenable than proceduralists for justifying disenfranchisement based on political incompetence. If democratic equality is a primary concern, the justifiability of child disenfranchisement is weakened (even through competence testing). In any case, child disenfranchisement can only be legitimate as long as the method for exclusion is not discriminatory, and as long as it tracks and restricts the right to vote to all individuals who do not meet the competence requirements, regardless of age.

Notes

1. 'Child', following the Convention on the Rights of the Child (CRC), is 'every human being below the age of 18 unless under the law applicable to the child, majority is attained earlier.' (UN General Assembly (UNGA), 1989, Art. 1). Used as synonymous of 'minor' or 'underage', as opposed to 'adult'. It includes all stages of development till majority (toddlers, children, teens and underage youths).
2. Argentina, Austria, Bosnia-Herzegovina, Brazil, Cuba, Ecuador, Nicaragua, Serbia, and Slovenia (as well as Germany and others for local elections; CIA (Central Intelligence Agency), 2020).
3. I limit the discussion to the justifiability of disenfranchising *citizens by their state.*
4. Some defenders of expanding the enfranchisement of children can also be included under this category (Cook, 2013; López-Guerra, 2012).
5. I thank Laura Lundy for hinting at the interpretative issues with Beckman's argument.
6. Thanks to an anonymous reviewer for encouraging me to clarify what is wrong with 'innocence'.
7. WEIRD: Western, Educated, Industrialised, Rich Democracies.
8. Many authors who endorse the expansion of franchise to children tend to rely on an outcomes-based understanding of democratic legitimacy. Through mathematical models (such as Condorcet's jury theorem) they attempt to prove that the inclusion of individuals who lack cognitive capacities to vote does not harm the outcome of the democratic process, thus, legitimate to include them (Goodin & Lau, 2011; Munn, 2018). To my knowledge, no author defends disenfranchisement exclusively based on outcomes. Thanks to an anonymous reviewer for requesting clarification.
9. Moral corruptness can be another trait that tracks harm through franchise; it seems to be the underlying principle behind the disenfranchisement of prisoners. This argument has not been used in the case of children. See debate in Beckman (2009: Ch.5).
10. Thanks to Marcus Häggrot for encouraging me to clarify how the Condorcet theorem fits into this argument.
11. Thanks to Dave Archard for encouraging me to frame it in this way.
12. Not all positions that rely on age thresholds defend the current age threshold as correct. Some, such as López-Guerra (2012) or Umbers (2020), consider current age thresholds as unjustified, arguing that the appropriate age of correlation to political competence would be between 10 and 12-years-old. This is a radical change if compared to the current system, but it still relies on the justifiability of statistical discrimination as a reason to (dis)enfranchise.
13. van Parijs (1998) also proposes a system for the disenfranchisement of the elderly.
14. Many authors show concern with competence-testing due to its practicalities (see, Rehfeld, 2011, p. 148–150; Clayton, 2006). There may be important pragmatic issues in determining the specific policy for a theory of enfranchisement, but they don't affect the (un)justifiability of disenfranchisement. As López-

Guerra argues (López-Guerra, 2012, p. 134), whether tests work better than alternative mechanisms for disenfranchisement (or against unconditional universal enfranchisement) depends on the institutional practices, public culture of and capacity to deter corruption in different societies.

Acknowledgments

I am indebted to the meticulous and enlightening editorial work of Marcus Carlsen Häggrot and Ben Boudou. Our discussions on various versions of this article improved it substantially. Thanks to Laura Lundy and Dave Archard as well for their thorough suggestions and comments.

Disclosure statement

No potential conflict of interest was reported by the author(s).

Funding

This work was supported by the British Academy Newton International Fellowship Grant No. NIFBA19\190492.

ORCID

Nico Brando http://orcid.org/0000-0003-1238-2205

References

Archard, D. (2004). *Children rights and childhood*. Routledge.
Archard, D., & Skivenes, M. (2009). Balancing a child's best interests and a child's views. *International Journal of Children's Rights*, *17*(1), 1–21. https://doi.org/10.1163/157181808X358276
Beckman, L. (2009). *The frontiers of democracy: The right to vote and its limits*. Palgrave Macmillan.
Beckman, L. (2018). Children and the right to vote. In A. Gheaus, G. Calder, & J. De Wispelaere (Eds.), *The routledge handbook of the philosophy of childhood and children* (pp. 479–491). Routledge.
Braconnier, C., Dormagen, J.-Y., & Pons, V. (2017). Voter registration costs and disenfranchisement: Experimental evidence from France. *American Political Science Review*, *111*(3), 584–604. https://doi.org/10.1017/S000305541700003X

Brando, N. (2020). Children's abilities, freedom, and the process of capability-formation. *Journal of Human Development and Capabilities, 21*(3), 249–262. https://doi.org/10.1080/19452829.2020.1767547

Brennan, J. (2011). The right to a competent electorate. *The Philosophical Quarterly, 61* (245), 700–724. https://doi.org/10.1111/j.1467-9213.2011.699.x

Brennan, J. (2016). *Against democracy*. Princeton University Press.

Caplan, B. (2006). *The myth of the rational voter*. Princeton University Press.

Chan, T. W., & Clayton, M. (2006). Should the voting age be lowered to sixteen? Normative and empirical considerations. *Political Studies, 54*(3), 533–558. https://doi.org/10.1111/j.1467-9248.2006.00620.x

Christiano, T. (2001). Knowledge and power in the justification of democracy. *Australasian Journal of Philosophy, 79*(2), 197–215. https://doi.org/10.1093/ajp/79.2.197

Christiano, T. (2002). Democracy as equality. In D. Estlund (Ed.), *Democracy*. Blackwell. 31–50.

CIA (Central Intelligence Agency) (2020). *The World Factbook: Suffrage*. At: https://www.cia.gov/library/publications/the-world-factbook/fields/311.html [May 8, 2020]

Clayton, M. (2006). *Justice and legitimacy in upbringing*. Oxford University Press.

Cook, P. (2013). Against a minimum voting age. *Critical Review of International Social and Political Philosophy, 16*(3), 439–458. https://doi.org/10.1080/13698230.2013.795707

Daniels, N. (1988). *Am I my parents' keeper? An essay on justice between the young and the old*. Oxford University Press.

Eekelaar, J. (1994). The interests of the child and the child's wishes: The role of dynamic self-determinism. *Journal of Law and the Family, 8*(1), 42–61. https://doi.org/10.1093/lawfam/8.1.42

Eekelaar, J., & Tobin, J. (2019). Art. 3 The best interests of the child. In J. Tobin (Ed.), *The UN convention on the rights of the child: A commentary*. Oxford University Press. 73–107.

Estlund, D. M. (2008). *Democratic authority: A philosophical framework*. Princeton University Press.

Fowler, T. (2014). The status of child citizens. *Politics, Philosophy & Economics, 13*(1), 93–113. https://doi.org/10.1177/1470594X13483482

Franklin, M. N. (2020). Consequences of lowering the voting age to 16: Lessons from comparative research. In J. Eichhorn & J. Bergh (Eds.), *Lowering the voting age to 16* (pp. 13–41). Palgrave Macmillan.

Gheaus, A. (2015). Unfinished adults and defective children: On the nature and value of childhood. *Journal of Ethics and Social Philosophy, 9*(1), 1–21. https://doi.org/10.26556/jesp.v9i1.85

Goodin, R. E. (2007). Enfranchising all affected interests, and its alternatives. *Philosophy & Public Affairs, 35*(1), 40–68. https://doi.org/10.1111/j.1088-4963.2007.00098.x

Goodin, R. E., & Lau, J. C. (2011). Enfranchising incompetents: Suretyship and the joint authorship of laws. *Ratio, 24*(2), 154–166. https://doi.org/10.1111/j.1467-9329.2011.00490.x

Hajnal, Z., Lajevardi, N., & Nielson, L. (2017). Voter identification laws and the suppression of minority votes. *Journal of Politics, 79*(2), 363–379. https://doi.org/10.1086/688343

Hinze, J. (2019). Does epistemic proceduralism justify the disenfranchisement of children? *Journal of Global Ethics*, *15*(3), 287–305. https://doi.org/10.1080/17449626.2019.1687569

Jarkovská, L., & Lamb, S. (2018). Not innocent, but vulnerable. In S. Lamb & J. Gilbert (Eds.), *The cambridge handbook of sexual development*. Cambridge University Press 76–93 .

Jenks, C. (2005). *Childhood*. Routledge.

Kolodny, N. (2014). Rule over none I: What justifies democracy? *Philosophy & Public Affairs*, *42*(3), 195–229. https://doi.org/10.1111/papa.12035

Lancy, D. F. (2015). *The anthropology of childhood. cherubs, chattel, changelings* (*Second Edition*. ed.). Cambridge University Press.

Lau, J. C. (2012). Two arguments for child enfranchisement. *Political Studies*, *60*(4), 860–876. https://doi.org/10.1111/j.1467-9248.2011.00940.x

Lister, R. (2007). Why citizenship: Where, when and how children? *Theoretical Inquiries in Law*, *8*(2), 693–718. https://doi.org/10.2202/1565-3404.1165

López-Guerra, C. (2012). Enfranchising minors and the mentally impaired. *Social Theory and Practice*, *38*(1), 115–138. https://doi.org/10.5840/soctheorpract20123815

Macleod, C. M. (2010). Primary goods, capabilities, and children. In H. Brighouse & I. Robeyns (Eds.), *Measuring Justice: Primary goods and capabilities* (pp. 174–192). Cambridge University Press.

Macleod, C. (2015). Agency, authority and the vulnerability of children. In A. Bagattini & C. Macleod (Eds.), *The nature of children's well-being: Theory and practice* (pp. 53–64). Springer.

Mahéo, V.-A., & Bélager, É. (2020). Lowering the voting age to 16?. *Canadian Journal of Political Science*. 53(3) , 596–617. https://doi.org/10.1017/S0008423920000232

Munn, N. J. (2012). Capacity testing the youth: A proposal for broader enfranchisement. *Journal of Youth Studies*, *15*(8), 1048–1062. https://doi.org/10.1080/13676261.2012.683406

Munn, N. J. (2018). Against the political exclusion of the incapable. *Journal of Applied Philosophy*, *35*(3), 601–616. https://doi.org/10.1111/japp.12229

Olsson, S. (2008). Children's suffrage: A critique of the importance of voters' knowledge for the well-being of democracy. *International Journal of Children's Rights*, *16*(1), 55–76. https://doi.org/10.1163/092755608X267120

Peto, T. (2018). Why the voting age should be lowered to 16. *Politics, Philosophy & Economics*, *17*(3), 277–297. https://doi.org/10.1177/1470594X17705651

Rehfeld, A. (2011). The child as democratic citizen. *The Annals of the American Academy of Political and Social Science*, *633*(1), 141–166. https://doi.org/10.1177/0002716210383656

Rutherford, J. (1997). One child, one vote: proxies for parents. *Minnesota Law Review*, *82*(6), 1463–1526. https://scholarship.law.umn.edu/mlr/1582

Schauer, F. (2018). Statistical (and non-statistical) discrimination. In K. Lippert-Rasmussen (Ed.), *The routledge handbook of the ethics of discrimination* (pp. 42–53). Routledge.

Schrag, F. (2004). Children and democracy: Theory and policy. *Politics, Philosophy & Economics*, *3*(3), 365–379. https://doi.org/10.1177/1470594X04046248

Skivenes, M. (2010). Judging the child's best interests: Rational reasoning or subjective presumptions? *Acta Sociologica*, *53*(4), 339–353. https://doi.org/10.1177/0001699310379142

Umbers, L. M. (2020). Enfranchising the youth. *Critical Review of International Social and Political Philosophy, 23*(6), 732–755. https://doi.org/10.1080/13698230.2018.1511172

UN General Assembly (UNGA) 1989. *Convention on the rights of the child*. Geneva: United Nations. Resolution 44/25 of November 20, 1989 in Geneva

van Parijs, P. (1998). The disfranchisement of the elderly, and other attempts to secure intergenerational justice. *Philosophy & public affairs, 27*(4), 292–333. https://doi.org/10.1111/j.1088-4963.1998.tb00072.x

Wagner, M., Johann, D., & Kritzinger, S. (2012). Voting at 16: Turnout and the quality of vote choice. *Electoral Studies, 31*(2), 372–383. https://doi.org/10.1016/j.electstud.2012.01.007

Weale, A. (1999). *Democracy*. Palgrave Macmillan.

Universal enfranchisement for citizens with cognitive disabilities – A moral-status argument

Regina Schidel

ABSTRACT

The social and cultural model of disability has challenged the historically powerful perception of disability as a deficiency. Disability is no longer conceived of solely in terms of an individual lack of capacities but also considered as a structural effect of disabling social institutions and normalizing thinking. The UN Convention on the Rights of Persons with Disabilities (CRPD) from 2006 marks a decisive step towards the recognition of humans with (cognitive) disabilities as legal subjects who are entitled to enjoy all human rights on equal terms with others. A central claim of the CRPD refers to full political participation of persons with (cognitive) disabilities. This paper argues for strengthening the political participation of persons with severe cognitive disabilities. The normative starting point is the claim that they are our equals, both morally and socially. In spelling out this status equality for the realm of the political, I focus on what political equality and inclusivity means concerning franchise. I will argue that the disenfranchisement of persons with cognitive disabilities, as practiced in many countries, cannot be justified. Furthermore, enfranchising persons with cognitive disabilities is deemed a central expression of their recognition as equals. Thus, it marks a crucial moment of emancipatory transformation towards a more inclusive political system. In cases where severely cognitive disabled persons cannot exercise the right to vote themselves, forms of assisted voting and supported decision-making must be available.

Introduction

For a long time, both in political theory and social practice, the view on persons with major cognitive disabilities has been dominated by a purely defective-oriented perspective. They have been at best perceived of as humans in need of treatment and as passive recipients of welfare means. Against this reductionist view, in this paper I defend the *egalitarian* position that persons with cognitive disabilities are full persons in a moral sense and that this equality of status must also manifest itself politically. As a central element of political equality, I propose that adult people with cognitive disabilities be fully enfranchised. 'Cognitive/intellectual disability' thereby refers for example, to forms of Down's syndrome, autism spectrum disorders or other mental handicaps that result in significantly limited opportunities for verbal and non-verbal communication. There has already been a decisive development of critically rethinking the former marginalization of persons with cognitive disabilities in political and legal theory (Barclay, 2018; Braun, 2015; Clifford Simplican, 2012; Fiala-Butora et al., 2014; López-Guerra, 2014; Mráz, 2020; Nussbaum, 2009, 2010; Palleit, 2013; Raad et al., 2009; Redley, 2008; Schriner et al., 1997; Schulte, 2012; Young, 2004). This strand of thought towards a more inclusive paradigm can be outlined along the unfolding of different models of 'disability'. I will briefly outline those different models to situate my argument within this conceptual landscape. Thereby it should get clear that thinking about disability is never solely descriptive but always already normatively impregnated.

The conventional mode of conceptualizing disability is often described as the *medical* model of disability, putting its focus on a 'normal' standard of human functioning (Wasserman et al., 2016). Judging disabled persons along the lines of their differing from medical norms, this model has mainly stressed their pathologies and shortcomings. Consequently, treatment and therapeutic interventions have been the most important instruments to deal with (cognitive) disability from the viewpoint of a medical perspective. The *social* (Silvers, 1998, p. 75) and *cultural* model of disability (Waldschmidt, 2017) has challenged this perception of disability in terms of illness and deficiency. Instead of looking at individual anomalies and malfunctioning, it focuses on social structures and patterns of consciousness that disabled persons in the first place and subject them to normalizing thinking (Butler, 2005). Thus, the social and cultural model marks a decisive shift in the understanding of disability: It is no longer conceived of in terms of an *individual* lack of capacities but as a *structural* effect of disabling social institutions and normalizing thinking. In this vein, 'ableism' is sometimes described as a discriminatory practice in analogy to racism or sexism. It refers to a problematic "network of beliefs, processes and practices that produces a particular kind of self and body [. . .] that is projected as the perfect, species-typical and therefore essential and fully human. Disability then is cast as a diminished state of being human." (Campbell, 2009, p. 5)

A third theoretical paradigm that tries to do justice to the complexity of disability and avoids the respective shortcomings of a purely medical or purely social-constructivist perspective, is the *human rights-based* model (Degener & Diehl, 2015). The central claim of the human rights-account of disability is a normative one: All persons, even those with severe cognitive and mental disabilities are our equals and share a common moral status of human beings. This shared moral status of all humans translates into fundamental claims concerning one's equality as member of political and legal communities. That is to say, the basic equality of one's moral status demands respect for one's status as political and legal subject on a par with others. In putting its focus on the moral and legal status of persons with disabilities, the human rights model can be read as combining the respective relevant insights of the medical and the socio-cultural model. It takes into account the special neediness of persons with disabilities in virtue of their physical or cognitive particularities. At the same time, it does not deny that disabilities are (at least in part) constructed by social barriers and structurally operative patterns of thinking. However, it is not limited to providing a diagnostic or critical approach to questions of disability but offers the resources for a discrete *normative egalitarian* argument.

The human rights approach to disability is realized in a paradigmatic way in the UN Convention on the Rights of Persons with Disabilities (CRPD) from 2006, which is binding for all nations that have ratified it. The CRPD can be interpreted as instance of recognizing humans with (cognitive) disabilities as equal persons and full legal subjects who are entitled to enjoy all human rights on equal terms with others.[1] Crucial for acknowledging persons with disabilities as equal legal subjects is Article 12 of the CRPD. It states that they ought to be equally recognized before the law.[2] The association of moral status equality and legal subjectivity as bearer of basic human rights has important *political* implications. It is a core element of democratic self-determination that all those subjected to political governance must have the opportunity to participate in it and must have an equal say in order to avoid arbitrary domination. Hence, counting as equal in moral and legal respect necessarily also means to be entitled to take part in democratic procedures and to be enfranchised equally.[3]

The specific question of voting rights for persons with cognitive disabilities has in recent years attracted some attention from political and legal theory scholars. Legal scholars have discussed the enfranchisement of persons with cognitive disabilities with reference to the human rights framework established by the CRPD (Braun, 2015; Fiala-Butora et al., 2014; Palleit, 2013; Schulte, 2012). In political theory and philosophy, by contrast, voting rights for intellectually disabled persons have been discussed as a step in broader arguments about voting rights for children (López-Guerra, 2012; Mráz, 2020), and some contributions have analysed the issue in terms of the moral status of cognitively disabled persons (Barclay, 2018; Nussbaum, 2010). In this essay, I follow this last line of thinking, but arrive at different practical conclusions than Barclay and Nussbaum. While Barclay argues that assisted voting may not be legalized due to status considerations, Nussbaum contends that substitutive voting should be accessible for persons with cognitive disabilities precisely in order to secure their equal status. I take up the status argument defended by both authors, however I advocate a position in between both of them in showing that Barclay's argument is too weak and that of Nussbaum overshot.

My argument proceeds as follows. At first, I reject a common preconception about legitimizing blanket disenfranchisement of persons with severe cognitive disabilities on epistemic grounds (I). Hereafter, I explicate the core normative argument for universal enfranchisement that refers to *status equality* of persons with cognitive disabilities in a moral and political sense. I argue that universal enfranchisement is a central element of status equality, regardless of whether one interprets voting rather as an expression of political self-determination or as aggregation of interests (II). On the grounds of this argument for status equality, I will defend universal enfranchisement against selective disenfranchisement based on capacity testing (III). In the final section, I argue that status equality demands that severely cognitively disabled persons have access to assisted decision-making (IV). I will close with a short conclusion.

Blanket disenfranchisement of persons with cognitive disabilities on epistemic grounds is unjustified

Some countries like Germany have until recently automatically deprived those persons of the right to vote for whom 'a custodian has been appointed [...] to attend to all his affairs' (Braun, 2015, p. 319). However, such blanket disenfranchisement of adult persons with cognitive disabilities who are under full legal custodianship is undermining their status as political equals and thereby cannot be justified. In this section I will approach this egalitarian argument from a *negative* perspective and refute a common preconception of how disenfranchisement could be legitimized. I argue that recourse to cognitive capacities or certain epistemic prerequisites is *not* sufficient to deny mentally disabled people the right to vote. Instead, if we conceive of political contributions in a broader and more pluralistic sense, it gets clearer that referring to presumed cognitive capacities cannot justify disenfranchisement.

In debates about democratic elections and the universal right to vote, we find the thesis that not only respecting the status of all citizens as equals, but also the quality of political decisions is central to it (Estlund, 2008). This quality of the results of democratic procedures and elections seems to presuppose a certain degree of cognitive capacity. But even if one admits that certain epistemic qualities are important for democratic decisions, there cannot be derived an argument about disenfranchisement from this. The burden of proof on the part of those who want to deny individuals the right to vote due to a presumed lack of epistemic or cognitive skills would be far too high. People with so-called intellectual disabilities have politically valuable contributions to make and increase the plurality of democratic procedures. Without giving a full-fledged justification for this, it suffices to underpin the argument of valuable contributions from a *negative* perspective. Denying the value of the contributions of persons with cognitive disabilities would presuppose a strong predefined understanding of rational political subjectivity, privileging it over other modes of political subjectivity. Yet, from an egalitarian perspective there are no convincing reasons for such a hierarchization. Therefore, this line of argument will allow for a more inclusive understanding of political subjectivity. I am only sketching this more inclusive understanding here to show that disenfranchisement based on cognitive and epistemic capacities of individuals cannot be justified.

The thesis is that people with intellectual disabilities definitely have *valuable political contributions* to make and increase the plurality and thus the legitimacy of political decisions. Failing to appreciate the political contributions of people with intellectual disabilities represents an epistemic injustice (Fricker, 2007) and points to an *ableist bias* in society. This ableist bias rests on a generalizing perception of severely cognitively disabled persons as incapable of political deliberation and participation. As this bias perpetuates a deficit-oriented view on persons with disabilities and undermines the normative aim of an inclusive society from the outset, it has to be philosophically deconstructed. On the contrary, it is crucial to stress that political deliberation and decision-making processes thrive on the plurality and diversity of those who contribute, as well as on the dissent that arises from the heterogeneity of perspectives. In light of the plurality of the members of a political community, it is precisely their heterogeneity that proves to be valuable and needs to be reconsidered. The exclusion of a group of adult members due to alleged incapacity is, against this background, merely an expression of an unjustifiable epistemic hierarchy.

This thesis may be solidified questioning a predefined form of *political subjectivity*. Often it is assumed that one has to be rational, reasonable and capable of intersubjective (verbal) communication in order to participate in joint procedures of political deliberation. Prima facie, this quite ambitious understanding of political capacity excludes at least some persons with severe cognitive disabilities, whose mental capacities do not allow them to exchange complex arguments and to participate in intellectually demanding forms of political decision-making. Disenfranchisement of adult persons with cognitive disabilities is inspired by the idea that participating in political procedures presupposes certain cognitive abilities. It is assumed that the quality of political procedures may profit from a certain level of rationality. Hence, a specific ideal of political subjectivity is presupposed. However, this is framed by a distorted and reduced image of political action and deliberation that should not remain uncontested. The automatic exclusion of cognitively disabled persons under full custodianship takes a particular understanding of what the right to vote consists of as its basis. It considers its active exercise as a farsighted and reasonable individual decision (Palleit, 2013, p. 316). Yet, this presupposes that there is an observer's perspective from where the relevant capacities for voting may be assessed.

I will shortly question this presupposition and will show that in defending a broader understanding of what political deliberation could amount to a predefined idealized picture of political subjectivity gets deconstructed. This argumentative move towards a pluralistic notion of forms of political participation and political subjectivity strengthens the possibility to interpret enfranchisement in a more inclusive way. Against presuming a knower's perspective from which persons' capacities to contribute meaningfully to political procedures may be judged, it is crucial to question a common understanding of deliberation in terms of an ideal speech situation (Habermas, 1993, p. 56). The ideal speech situation presupposes perfectly rational agents who compete for better arguments and thereby observe a number of argumentative rules. Habermas' theory claims to include all persons who are affected by the outcome of a political decision in the deliberative process. However, such demanding requirements for political discourse are highly excluding as they rest on the ideal of autonomous and fully reasonable deliberators. Such an idealized understanding should be replaced by a broadened conception as it is for example, represented in feminist theory (Benhabib, 1994; Fraser, 1990; Phillips, 1998; Young, 2011). Thereby also acts of public appearance or joint speech may count as forms of political deliberation. A correspondingly revised notion of political subjectivity allows for a broader and more pluralistic conception of the citizen as bearer of the right to vote.

Against this backdrop other forms of how political deliberation could be thought of. Clifford Simplican for example, proposes a model that she calls 'collaborative speech' (Clifford Simplican, 2012, p. 221). This model defends a broad notion of public deliberation and includes forms of non-verbal participation and bodily presence as variants of deliberative practices. Persons with cognitive disabilities who cannot communicate verbally are thereby enabled to participate in political procedures.[4] Clifford describes collaborative speech

> as a way to integrate the political needs of individuals who have little ability to articulate their own demands. Collaborative speech recognizes the multiple and profound ways that deliberants are reciprocally dependent on one another, both in the ways in which needs are constructed and how listeners interpret those needs. (Clifford Simplican, 2012, p. 220)

She cites the example of Sue and Charlie Swenson, a disability activist and her adult son who has physical and cognitive disabilities, who attended together the consultations for the UN Convention on the Rights of Persons with

Disabilities in New York. Clifford argues that both Charlie's bodily presence and his non-verbal communicating via grunting and his presence together with his mother representing their interdependency was a decisive contribution to the delegation's counselling that could not have been substituted by an advocate's speech:

> By his body, grunts and surrounded by his support team, Charlie expressed a wide array of needs that the delegation had formally neglected. By advocating together, the Swenson delegation upturns the conviction that agents are best able to represent their needs autonomously. (Clifford Simplican, 2012, p. 221)

Thus, two elements emerge as possible variations of deliberation: the mere presence of persons like Charlie who are normally invisible in public deliberation, even if their matters are on stake and the manifestation of forms of interdependency and reciprocal representation.

An approach similar to Clifford's of how we could extend and modify our understanding of deliberation is given by Thomas Schramme. He describes deliberation as a practice of joint effort that can only be realized when heterogeneous perspectives interact. As he defends a broad understanding of what deliberation means, it does not necessarily presuppose certain capacities (e.g. that for language), but relies on the interplay of a variety of contributions:

> [I] in the joint effort model of deliberation people with minority minds can be fully participating deliberators, because not all individual deliberators need to have roughly the same deliberative skills, as in the competitive intellectual model. It is not required to participate in an intellectually demanding style." (Schramme, 2021, p. 6)

Thus, a look at joint deliberation and its need for a heterogeneity of viewpoints highlights how deliberation profits from 'minority minds' as they burst standardized patterns of political thinking and contribute different and fruitful experiences and needs. Therefore, a meaningful conceptualization of political participation, which is able to take into account the plurality of a community, cannot (exclusively) rely on individual cognitive capacities, but has to focus much more on joint decision-making and bodily forms of communication and presence. If political participation cannot be limited to an ideal discourse situation but is thought of in a more broad and pluralistic way, this also leads to a revised image of the citizen as a voter. This revised picture of political subjectivity underlines the unjustifiability of disenfranchising adults with cognitive disabilities. This means that a regulation according to which persons under custodianship in all affairs are automatically disenfranchised is highly unjust.[5]

The criticism of a predefined form of political subjectivity shows why recourse to cognitive capacities of individuals cannot justify blanket disenfranchisement of a group of citizens, even if one sticks to the epistemic quality as decisive element of democratic procedures. Deconstructing a predefined understanding of epistemic quality makes clear that doubting the capacity of persons with cognitive disabilities to contribute meaningfully to political issues is unjustified.[6] In the next section I will further elaborate on status equality as *affirmative* reason of why adult persons with cognitive disabilities should universally be enfranchised.

Defending universal enfranchisement as expression of the equal status of persons with cognitive disabilities

Defending full political participation and universal enfranchisement for persons with severe cognitive disabilities rests on the premise that they share an *equal moral status* with all human beings. This equality in moral respect implies full legal subjectivity and full participatory parity in political affairs. The nexus between moral and legal/political equality refers to the practical dimension of respecting humans as equals: It has to become manifest in the relations of persons living together in communities. Namely, in the way how they organise their common affairs and treat each other reciprocally. This relevance of intersubjectively recognizing each other as equals who owe each other respect is captured by accounts of *social relational equality* (Anderson, 1999; Scheffler, 2003; Schemmel, 2015). Their focus is not on contingent and factual inequalities between persons. Instead, they stress their normatively assumed equality:

> „[Equality] is, [. . .] a moral ideal governing the relations in which people stand to one another. [. . .] [T]his ideal abstracts from the undeniable differences among people. It claims that human relations must be conducted on the basis of an assumption that everyone's life is equally important, and that all members of a society have equal standing. (Scheffler, 2003, pp. 21f.)

This comparative notion of relational equality of all members of a political community displays a *material* and an *expressive* dimension (Mráz, 2020, pp. 268 f.). The 'Material Requirement of Political Equality' refers to reconsidering each person's politically relevant interests and issues and their participatory contribution to political decision-making. The 'Expressive Requirement of Political Equality' refers to the symbolic dimension of manifesting one's status as equal being: '[N]o member of the political community should be subject to any treatment by the community that expresses their moral inequality or lesser worth as members of the political community.' (Mráz, 2020, p. 268)

It is not necessary here to justify and deduce the notion of *moral equality* underlying political equality in a comprehensive way, e. g. starting from a philosophical conception of human dignity. Instead of giving a full-fledged *positive* account of why all human beings have equal moral status,

I proceed from a *critical-negative* perspective. It rests on the hypothesis that no one may assume the authority to attribute moral status to some (groups) of persons and to deny it others. Thereby one would take a normative-epistemic standpoint 'from nowhere' for granted, a 'god's trick' (Haraway, 1988, p. 581) that lacks any justificatory grounding since it presupposes a neutral-objective perspective on normative standing that is opposed to human's embeddedness as situated relational beings and their co-dependency. Decisive for such a critical and negatively operating account of human status equality is the renunciation to refer to any individual capacities or properties that would explain why human beings are to be respected as equals. An anti-essentialist approach to human equality has rather to take seriously the idea that human equality is founded in a shared human condition (Arendt, (1998) [1958]). Judith Butler has recently elaborated on the idea of human interdependency and vulnerability to each other as a starting point for claiming social equality (Butler, 2020). She shows that a shared vulnerability constitutes human beings as fundamentally dependent on each other. This shared condition already implies a normative requirement for recognition and mutual dependency: "[I]nterdependency, though accounting for differentials of independence and dependence, implies social equality: each is dependent, or formed and sustained in relations of depending upon, and being depended upon" (Butler, 2020, p. 16). *Because* human beings are interconnected in physical, psychic and social terms, they owe each other reciprocal respect. Although this claim to respect that Butler grasps as 'social equality' is meant to be universal, she is totally aware of the fact that social realty is deeply shaped by disparities and violent devaluations that uphold an unequal valuing of human lives. These unequal valuations of human life and the status hierarchies produced thereby are to be criticized from the standpoint of human relationality and interwovenness. This critique reveals an epistemic point of view from 'inside' humans' dependency on each other that forecloses any possibility to ascribe some persons a higher moral status than others. Thus, taking seriously human interdependence and relationality as source of a fundamental normative claim, cannot mean to reify groups of persons as subaltern, deficient or especially needy and to thereby produce paternalistic hierarchies. On the contrary, such an immanent standpoint from the midst of human relationality allows for proclaiming radical equality in a normative sense, while at the same time being aware of existing hierarchies and inequalities.

With respect to severely cognitive disabled persons this affirmation of moral and social equality means that they have to be respected as equals, both in material as well as expressive regards. But this status equality of all persons – and here the focus is on those with cognitive disabilities – is permanently undermined in current societies. Treating them as unequal does not just concern political matters and social affairs like school education and the labour market, but also one-sided stereotypes and problematic patterns of (non-)recognition. Such demeaning modes of perception, which frame cognitive disabled persons as childlike, inferior or flawed undermine their equality mainly in an *expressive* sense and can be understood in terms of 'epistemic injustice' (Fricker, 2007) as their valuable contributions are underestimated or simply ignored. Framed in the language of recognition theory, one could speak of epistemic exclusion through misrecognition and problematic subjectivations (Butler, 2005). To conceive of cognitively disabled persons first and foremost as cognitively disabled means to reduce them to their deficiencies and impairments. It defines subjects mainly through their disability.[7]

This structural perspective on how persons with cognitive disabilities are stigmatized through comparison with standards of 'normality' underlines the importance of empowering their status as political equals. One grave infringement of status equality in the realm of the political is disenfranchisement of persons with severe cognitive disabilities. Disenfranchisement is on the one hand undermining the standing as equals defended in this section and on the other hand is perpetuating the structural misrecognition of persons with cognitive disabilities as political subjects. Against that, universal enfranchisement fosters political equality both in material and expressive respect and thereby destabilizes the denigration of cognitively disabled persons.[8]

Against the backdrop of the described normalizing tendencies and the denigration of people with intellectual disabilities in our society, one possibility would be to outline an inclusive political system that looks radically different from current democracies. However, I pursue a more limited aim here and ask how our current democratic systems could presently take into account people with intellectual disabilities and recognize their status as equals, both in material and expressive regards. Yet, this approach is connected with a critical and deconstructive moment towards problematic practices of devaluation and the political exclusion of people with intellectual disabilities. The universalization of enfranchisement for people with cognitive disabilities creates a moment of critical difference to existing forms of exclusion and inequality. In one paradigmatic case of political participation, equality of status and thus a moment of political inclusiveness is implemented which implicates a transgressive and transformative dimension of 'not yet': Enfranchising persons with cognitive disabilities marks one crucial stance towards full political participation of those who have been formerly unrepresented. The partial realization of something that has not yet been realized as a whole (the political inclusion of persons with cognitive disabilities) opens up a critical difference to present practices of exclusion and thus serves an emancipatory aim. As in case of women's suffrage in the early decades of the 20th century, it embodies one decisive step of breaking up existing social and political inequalities and thereby opens up a critical distance towards them, outlining contours of that what could be possible in the future. Thus, enfranchisement as expression of political equality is a crucial element of participatory parity (Fraser, 1990) in collective self-determination.

The right to vote constitutes a central human right that should be enjoyed by all adult persons of a political community. Arendt therefore characterizes franchise and eligibility for office as 'only political rights' that 'constitute in a modern democracy the very quintessence of citizenship' (Arendt, 1959, p. 51) and Waldron even links enfranchisement to the status of equal *dignity* of all persons (Waldron, 2012, p. 38). Democratic voting thus constitutes a central form of political participation in collective self-determination, that is to say the enactment of public autonomy:

> The right to vote, interpreted as a positive liberty, becomes the paradigm for rights in general not just because it is constitutive for political self-determination but because its structure allows one to see how inclusion in a community of equal members is connected with the individual entitlement to make autonomous contributions and take positions of one's own. (Habermas, 1998, p. 271)

Universal enfranchisement as expression of status equality is thereby not dependent on how one interprets the meaning of democratic voting exactly. Regardless of whether it is understood rather as form of enactment of one's political autonomy or rather as bringing in one's political interests, it is decisive in stressing one's status as equal political authority. I will briefly outline the two dimensions and then argue that both hint towards the material and expressive status equality of all adult members of a political community.

One interpretation of the right to vote defines it as an individual public right through which citizens exercise their political freedom of democratic self-government (Badura, 1987, p. 957; Funke, 2007, p. 396). This characterization alludes prima facie to the understanding of voting as the enactment of political autonomy by the citizen who acts in an enlightened, mature and competent manner (Palleit, 2013, p. 316). In a similar vein, López-Guerra speaks of 'the moral and rational aptitude to rank political alternatives according to some criterion and choose accordingly' (López-Guerra, 2012, p. 131) that has to be presupposed for enfranchisement. The ideal of an enlightened and democratically responsible use of one's right to vote based on profound knowledge of the electoral system and the election programs of political parties is of course quite attractive. However, it cannot provide a theoretical justification for limiting enfranchisement. As various scholars highlight, democratic voting allows for the possibility to vote irrationally or in a manner that is democratically imprudent (Braun, 2015, p. 339). Palleit emphasizes that it builds one of the most basic achievements of modern democracy that the voting act of each citizen has to be accepted equally, independent of personal reasons or motives (Palleit, 2013, pp. 316 f.). Hence, the interpretation of the right to vote as an expression of political autonomy can only make sense if this autonomy is not interpreted in the strict sense of a quantitatively pre-defined empirical ability leading to the exclusion of those who are denied the capacity of reasonable political self-determination. Instead, the moment of political self-determination via the enactment of one's vote has to be interpreted differently. The point is that adults with cognitive disabilities count as equal co-authors of a political community and have an equal say. Even if they make an imprudent use of their vote – a possibility that is in no way limited to persons with cognitive disabilities – it has to be respected as enactment of their political autonomy.

A second interpretation of what voting means highlights that citizens express their political interests during elections and thereby insert them into political decision-making (Funke, 2007, p. 399). This interest-based model rather stands for the aggregation of individual concerns without a deliberative process that transforms them into a common political will.[9] Thereby one need not assume a certain kind of political subjectivity in form of perfect rational deliberators, but just that citizens have relevant interests that should be considered insofar as they are affected by political decisions and actions. With regard to severely cognitively disabled persons, it cannot be denied that they have political interests that are underrepresented in public discourse. Here it is also important to note that persons with cognitive disabilities do not just have interests that concern their disabilities. Instead, they have interests in all sorts of regards. For example, they too can be eco-sensitive, feminist or cultural conservative. We should concede that point, even when those interests and concerns are not always fully accessible, communicable or understandable. Otherwise, granting equal political status without the assumption of material political interests would be in some way senseless. Sometimes persons with severe cognitive disabilities cannot speak for themselves and articulate their viewpoints or are made publicly invisible and unheard through structures of exclusion. But that doesn't make their political interests less meaningful or worth of consideration. Consequently, as they are affected by political processes and law-making, they have an interest in being involved and reconsidered.[10] Goodin, who defends an interest model of enfranchisement, supports this view but highlights the difficulty of how the interests of the 'mental incompetents' may be taken into consideration:

> It is not as if those interests are less deserving of consideration. It is merely that their carriers cannot, for one reason or another, speak for themselves in pressing those interests politically. What is absurd is to suggest that they can – to suggest that we could read votes off the babbling of infants or of streams,

> either. But the absurdity of that suggestion does not translate into any absurdity in the idea that their interests ought to be represented, by others as necessary. (Goodin, 1996, p. 841)

Goodin's point is justified in so far as certain cognitive capacities are necessary to be able to articulate one's political interests or to decide which representatives might realize one's interests at best. However, that does not mean – as he rightly stresses – that persons with cognitive disabilities did not have those interests. Representing them by others should by no means be a default solution, since it undermines agency and autonomy that persons with cognitive disabilities most often have. Therefore, assistance in articulating one's interests is preferable to mere substitution.

My point in sketching those two strands of how to interpret the exact content of the right to vote is not to defend one of them against the other. Rather I want to show that neither of them can be used to deny status equality and enfranchisement of persons with cognitive disabilities. Both aspects are relevant for people with intellectual disabilities, since both affirm their *status* as equal members of a political community. Enfranchising persons with cognitive disabilities articulates the promise that they might be respected as co-authors of a political community (the public autonomy component), whereas the interest component hints to the demand that the concerns of disabled persons count equally in social and political life. Both the political autonomy as well as the interest dimension are decisive for enfranchising persons with cognitive disabilities since both refer back to the expressive meaning of counting as equal member of a political community. On the one hand, the right to vote offers the possibility to take part in political processes on an equal basis with others so as to perform one's political autonomy – whereby this concept should not be understood in a too demanding and intellectualist way. On the other hand, voting is a possibility to express one's interests in the political context.

So, both possible interpretations of what democratic voting exactly consists in – whether as common deliberative self-determination of a community or as the possibility to contribute specific interests and viewpoints – hint towards the *expressive* dimension of having the status of an equal in moral and political regards. The potential stigma of being excluded from political procedures, in which all other adult citizens of a community are involved, does not only consist in having no voice. More than that, it also rests in another experience that, symbolically speaking, is possibly even more serious – namely, the experience of being devalued and excluded in a social hierarchy. Thus, universal enfranchisement is crucial for critically resisting social and political inequalities and denigrations (Haslanger, 2013). Granting persons with cognitive disabilities universal enfranchisement represents an affirmative moment of difference towards problematic practices of exclusion. Properly implemented, it constitutes a decisive moment of inclusion for persons with cognitive disabilities and thereby reveals a transformative potential aiming at realizing political equality.

Defending universal enfranchisement against selective disenfranchisement

So far, my argument has shown that the right to vote as a central political right is crucial for realizing status equality of all citizens of a community in both material and expressive terms. I therefore advocate granting people with cognitive disabilities, as well as all other adult citizens of a community, the right to vote – regardless of the presumed absence or presence of individual cognitive properties. Enfranchisement is a central requirement of political equality. It enables the members of a political community to actively participate in the shaping of common affairs in material regards. Moreover, it also comprises a more symbolic dimension, namely to be considered as an equal authority. I do not implicate thereby that enfranchising persons with cognitive disabilities would realize their social and political equality in a comprehensive way. Rather, it exemplifies just one central dimension of political inclusivity. However, in implementing status equality in this central domain of political participation a critical distance towards existing inequalities is revealed and an emancipatory potential that rests to be redeemed gets manifest.

Regarding the right to vote, it has been common to disenfranchise persons with severe cognitive disabilities until the most recent past. Elsewhere, a form of 'capacity testing' has been introduced in order not to exclude all those under full legal custodianship from the right to vote. However, both forms of restricting enfranchisement with regard to severely cognitively disabled persons are highly problematic, since they likewise undermine their recognition as equals. Both are based on a reduced understanding of politically relevant cognitive abilities and presuppose a pre-defined notion of political participation and thus reproduce an ableist bias.

In contrast to disenfranchisement in the case of full custodianship, that I refuted in section I, capacity-testing could be prima facie regarded as justified. It does not exclude a whole group of persons from the right to vote but takes the individual person and her capacities into account. However, capacity-testing is normatively problematic as well. Barclay refers to the case of the US state of Maine where the federal district court laid out the criteria that should be applied in determining each individual's entitlement to vote in 2001 (Barclay, 2018, p. 121). The Competence Assessment Tool for Voting (CAT-V), devised on the basis of the court's demands, 'asks individuals a set of basic questions designed to test that they understand what voting is (that people go to mark their vote on a form), and what effect voting has (that the person with the most votes wins).' (Barclay, 2018, p. 121)

As Barclay stresses, it is highly discriminating to support a 'partial franchise' of cognitively disabled persons on individual assessments of capacity (Barclay, 2018, p. 118). She argues that such a testing regime would have enormous costs regarding the equal status of persons with disabilities, even if they pass the test:

> What a profoundly damaging public statement to make of someone who is singled out for testing that hardly anyone else is subject to! [...] While most people with cognitive disabilities will pass any non-discriminatory test for voting capacity, they will still understand that they have been singled out for testing that most others are not subject to [...] Capacity testing represents a clear threat to their standing as equals. (Barclay, 2018, p. 122)

The problem with capacity testing is its stigmatizing character: To be singled out for the testing procedure can be regarded as symbolic harm and can thus undermine the expressive dimension of status equality. Persons with cognitive disabilities are thus subjected to the necessity to prove their capacity for exercising a fundamental right that others just have without further need to demonstrate their ability. In consequence, capacity testing would undermine the character of the right to vote as a basic *right* and turn it into a *privilege* (Braun, 2015, p. 340). This does also preclude the possibility that a judge or physician would decide about individual enfranchisement: The former European Commissioner for Human Rights says about the CRPD:

> [It] leaves no room for procedures in which judges or medical practitioners would assess the voting competence of a person and then give a green light – or not. As we do not test that capability for someone without disabilities, this would amount to blatant discrimination. (Hammarberg, 2011).

Since capacity testing violates the material dimension of political equality, but to an even greater extent also the expressive dimension of status equality, it should be rejected. Something like a rationality test would define what can and cannot be considered as a politically meaningful contribution and is therefore to be rejected from the outset. Thereby such a notion of a rationality test submits to a pre-defined notion of political subjectivity that is no compatible with respect for status equality of all members of a political community.

Assisted decision-making vs. substitutive voting

I have argued that disenfranchising people with intellectual disabilities is a violation of their equality of status. Moreover, it should also be rejected from the perspective of a plural and heterogeneous understanding of politics. What follows from this philosophical argument in practical regards?

Having rejected the possibilities to exclude persons with cognitive disabilities from the right to vote on grounds of custodianship in all affairs, capacity testing or a pre-defined ideal of political subjectivity, it seems difficult how their disenfranchisement can be justified. The universal enfranchisement for all persons with disabilities, just as proclaimed by the CRPD, must thus be defended as a question of political status equality. This has to provide the background for considering how persons so cognitively disabled that they cannot exercise their right to vote alone could be given the best possible assistance. I cannot give a full-blown account of voting assistance here but will offer some prospective thoughts on the basis of taking status equality seriously. The point I pursue thereby is that there are practical ways to enable most persons with cognitive disabilities to vote if assistance is available.

Barclay makes an argument for universal enfranchisement for cognitively disabled persons that places a constraint on the practical exercise of the voting procedure in person:

> We should deny people assistance when casting their vote. A person with cognitive disabilities, like everyone else, will be legally entitled to vote. They should enjoy proper opportunities to discuss the election with others, to ask questions, and to receive accessible information about the election and how to vote [. . .]. But when it comes to actually casting a vote, all people should be required to do so on their own. (Barclay, 2018, p. 123)

Barclay aims at securing the principle of 'one person one vote' and at avoiding the possibilities of undue influence or manipulation (Schriner et al., 1997, p. 92) through this constraint. However, her constraint seems overshot: many electoral systems allow for postal vote and assistance in voting to secure the possibility to cast their vote for those who may not be able for whatever reasons to mark the ballot paper in the polling booth themselves. Though, Barclay's argument against assisted voting has a point insofar as it seems practically impossible to draw a sharp line between assisted voting and substitutive voting. To what extent is the assisted voter influenced by the person supporting him? And what if the proxy votes on the basis of the reconstructed interest of her ward? The decisive difference between autonomous voting and proxy voting cannot consist in who actually draws the cross on the ballot paper. This is rather obvious if we just think of a paralysed person who instructs her assistant where to mark the vote or if we imagine the case of a person with dementia who fills in the ballot paper herself but does so according to the instructions of her child. Nonetheless, it makes sense to distinguish between *substitutive* and *assisted voting*. The first means that a proxy actually votes in the place of the represented person and reconstructs their presumed political interest without the represented person being involved in the voting process. The second refers to cases when a disabled person informs the representative of her choice which party or candidate to vote for on her behalf or gets assistance in doing so. It is important to note that in assisted voting the person with cognitive disabilities is herself part of the decision process.

To avoid the exclusion of persons with cognitive disabilities from elections who cannot vote themselves or communicate their preferences, Nussbaum defends the possibility of substitutive voting (Nussbaum, 2010, p. 91). She argues that manipulation by a guard is no less probable if we assume that guardians usually act responsibly than the possibility that the vote of persons is influenced by parents, spouses or their pastor (Nussbaum, 2010, p. 91). In balancing the possible dangers of substitutive voting against the effects and meaning of disenfranchisement, Nussbaum rejects the second option:

> What is the alternative? That, as at present, a large group of citizens are simply disqualified from the most essential functions of citizenship. They do not count. Their interests are not weighed in the balance. That, to me, means that they are not regarded as fully equal citizens with a dignity commensurate with that of others. (Nussbaum, 2010, p. 91)

For the evaluation of assisted and substitutive voting it is central to refer to the considerations made above on equality of status and to take the relationship between material and expressive equality as starting point for an assessment in this regard. The normative argument for status equality pursued so far in this article should have made clear that forms of assisted voting have to be available for persons with cognitive disabilities. In contrast, the question of whether substitutive voting should be allowed is much more difficult to answer.

At the center of the justification for an inclusive interpretation of the right to vote is the status argument. The right to vote is a legally guaranteed implementation of the political equality of status. With the interpretation of the right to vote as an expression of status equality, I do not commit myself to the exact meaning of political elections and the exercise of the right to vote. I have argued that this can involve both the element of political participation on par with others and the input of one's own politically relevant interests. To put it another way: To be regarded as politically equal authority implies not only the possibility of being actively involved in the common shaping of the political order but concerns the ability to articulate one's own interests and let them become politically effective.

Since granting the right to vote cannot be linked to giving proof of certain rational and cognitive abilities, people with intellectual disabilities must not be deprived of the right to vote in general. Rather, it must be ensured that assistance and the necessary technical aids are available to them to exercise their right to vote. Assistance in exercising the right to vote can be understood broadly: Just as many people only come to a voting decision through discussion and exchange and are influenced by reasons that others express, the political choice of a person with intellectual disabilities always takes place in a social and intersubjective context. Since people with cognitive disabilities are particularly vulnerable and susceptible to abusive and paternalistic attacks, it must be ensured that they are only assisted in exercising their right to vote and that the voting decision is not taken over by the assisting person.

Conceptually, it is extremely difficult to pinpoint the line between assistance and substitution. I propose the following determination: The exercise of the right to vote is *assisted* if the will and the political interests of the person concerned are expressed in the voting decision and they themselves articulate this decision – through whatever forms of communication that do not have to be necessarily verbal. On the contrary, *substitutive* voting takes place when the person with intellectual disabilities themselves is not directly involved in the election, but their deputy reconstructs their decision based on their interests or concerns (as best as possible), but ultimately makes this decision instead of the person represented.

While the assisted exercise of the right to vote must be made possible in any case, it is highly questionable whether substitutive voting should be legalized for persons who by no means can communicate their voting decision to their assistant. Beyond the difficulty of properly reconstructing the political interests of the disabled person, we face a risk of paternalistic and abusive practice since there is no guarantee that proxies would actually vote in the interest of their wards. Moreover, it is not clear, whether status equality of people with intellectual disabilities would be preserved or rather undermined if others decide on their behalf. There remains the theoretical as well as practical desideratum of spelling out ways how assisted voting could take place that does not produce false results, that is to say an electoral decision the supporter falsely judges to be the will of the represented person.

Conclusion

I have started my reflections on how political representation and specifically enfranchisement of the severely cognitively disabled could look like based on contrasting a medical, a social/cultural and a human rights-based model of disability. It seems that neither of them is all-encompassing concerning the question of political participation, but each contributes important aspects: the medical model (although reductive taken by itself) calls attention to the fact that persons with (cognitive) disabilities are especially vulnerable and in need of different sorts of support and resources. The social and cultural model reveal our common stereotypes and ascriptions about persons with cognitive disabilities and offer the possibility to question how we think about political deliberation traditionally. Finally, the human rights model of disability which highlights the legal subjectivity of all persons, even those with severe cognitive disabilities, directs the focus away from conceiving of them as welfare recipients but stresses their status as equal bearers of human rights and as political equals instead.

This equality of status in political terms depends on granting universal enfranchisement in order to foster both the material and the expressive dimension of counting as equals. The question of whether other forms of representing the political regards of persons with cognitive disabilities like an ombudsperson in parliament would be helpful rests to be further examined.

Notes

1. The CRPD does not favour a purely medical neither a purely social perspective on disability, but puts forward an intersectional understanding defining persons with disabilities as 'those who have long-term physical, mental, intellectual or sensory impairments which in interaction with various barriers may hinder their full and effective participation in society on an equal basis with others.' (CRPD, Article 1). Thereby it accounts both for social mechanisms of disabling and stigmatizing structures.
2. Several authors interpret this fundamental human right to legal equality to involve two central aspects: Firstly, it marks a right to legal capacity. That means being an authority that according to Hannah Arendt's formulation has 'the right to have rights' (Arendt, 1976, p. 296). Secondly, this fundamental right also entails the claim to exercise this legal capacity (Aichele & von Bernstorff, 2010; Palleit, 2013). The idea that human rights cannot be reduced to their character as negative liberal rights but have an activating dimension as 'entitlements to capabilities' is highlighted in Sen's theory (Sen, 2005, pp. 152ff.). Thereby not only the normative notion of being an equal legal authority is put forward, but also the political and social perspective of performing one's legal agency.
3. Habermas defends the co-originality of democratic self-determination and basic individual rights: The „internal connection between popular sovereignty and human rights lies in the normative content of the very mode of exercising political autonomy." (Habermas, 1998, p. 103) I cannot discuss the nexus between legal subjectivity and political autonomy here in more detail but proceed from Habermas' theory.
4. For the concept of a politics of presence cf., Phillips (1998).
5. There are further reasons why disenfranchising persons under full legal custodianship is illegitimate and undermines status equality: Trusteeship for persons with cognitive disabilities is not designated to deprive the wards of their rights. Rather more, it aims at guaranteeing proper exercise of those rights and at supporting the fulfilment of the wards' financial concerns, health issues or housing matters. (Braun, 2015, p. 325; Schulte, 2012, p. 18).
6. The violation of status equality in case of disenfranchisement even outweighs supposedly losses of epistemic quality. Mráz argues convincingly that there might be capacity-based reasons for not allowing children to vote in general, but that this argument does not apply in the case of people with intellectual disabilities, for both empirical and normative considerations. Adults with intellectual disabilities represent a very small quantitative group and it is highly unlikely that they will negatively affect the quality of democratic decisions. At

the same time, having no right to vote does not constitute a violation of the status of children, since their equality is not harmed in *comparative* terms, whereas this is very much so in the case of adults with intellectual disabilities (Mráz, 2020, pp. 274 f.).

7. The question how to address persons with cognitive disabilities without stigmatizing them through this categorization needs further discussion and consideration.
8. This argument does not imply that universalizing enfranchisement would automatically eliminate all forms of stigmatizing and inequality that persons with cognitive disabilities face. But it marks a decisive step in including persons with cognitive disabilities in political processes and strengthening their standing as equals on a par with others. Thus, it reveals a transformative emancipatory potential.
9. My portrayal of an interest vs. a political autonomy approach of voting does of course not claim to mirror the whole bunch of theories about enfranchisement and the meaning of voting – I have not mentioned republican approaches or those inspired by discourse theory.
10. Cf. the "all-affected interests' principle', Goodin (2007), p. 50.

Acknowledgments

For valuable critique and ideas on different versions of this essay, I am especially grateful to Benjamin Boudou, Ali Emre Benli and Marcus Häggrot. For thoroughly reading and commenting I thank Ronan Kaczynski and Jasper Kunstreich.

Disclosure statement

No potential conflict of interest was reported by the author(s).

References

Aichele, V., & von Bernstorff, J. (2010). Das Menschenrecht auf gleiche Anerkennung vor dem Recht: Zur Auslegung von Art. 12 der UN-Behindertenrechtskonvention. *Betreuungsrechtliche Praxis*, *5*, 199–203.

Anderson, E. S. (1999). What is the point of equality? *Ethics*, *109*(2), 287–337. https://doi.org/10.1086/233897

Arendt, H. ((1998) [1958]). *The human condition (With a preface by Margaret Canovan)*. University of Chicago Press.

Arendt, H. (1959). Reflections on little rock. *Dissent*, *6*(1), 45–56.

Arendt, H. (1976). *The Origins of Totalitarianism*. (New Edition with Added Prefaces). Harcourt Brace. University of Chicago Press.

Badura, P. (1987). Die parlamentarische Demokratie. In P. Kirchhof & J. Isensee (Eds.), *Handbuch des Staatsrechts der Bundesrepublik Deutschland* (pp. 953–986). C. F. Müller Juristischer Verlag.
Barclay, L. (2018). *Disability with dignity. Justice, human rights and equal status.* Routledge.
Benhabib, S. (1994). Deliberative rationality and models of democratic legitimacy. *Constellations, 1*(1), 26–52. https://doi.org/10.1111/j.1467-8675.1994.tb00003.x
Braun, K. (2015). "Nothing about us without us": The legal disenfranchisement of voters with disabilities in germany and its compliance with international human rights standards on disabilities. *American University International Law Review, 30*(2), 315–346.
Butler, J. (2005). *Giving an Account of Oneself.* Fordham University Press.
Butler, J. (2020). *The force of nonviolence: The ethical in the political.* Verso.
Campbell, F. K. (2009). *Contours of ableism.* Palgrave Macmillan UK.
Clifford Simplican, S. (2012). Making disability public in deliberative democracy. *Contemporary Political Theory, 11*(2), 211–228. https://doi.org/10.1057/cpt.2011.11
Degener, T., & Diehl, E. (Ed.). (2015). *Handbuch Behindertenrechtskonvention: Teilhabe als Menschenrecht – Inklusion als gesellschaftliche Aufgabe.* Bundeszentrale für Politische Bildung.
Estlund, D. M. (2008). *Democratic authority: A philosophical framework.* Princeton University Press.
Fiala-Butora, J., Stein, M. A., & Lord, J. E. (2014). The democratic life of the union: toward equal voting participation for europeans with disabilities. *Harvard International Law Journal, 55*(1), 71–104.
Fraser, N. (1990). Rethinking the public sphere: A contribution to the critique of actually existing democracy. *Social Text, 25*(26), 56–80. https://doi.org/10.2307/466240
Fricker, M. (2007). *Epistemic injustice: Power and the ethics of knowing.* Oxford University Press.
Funke, A. (2007). Wahlrecht, Republik, Politische Freiheit: Zur Begründung des Rechts auf Wahl nach Art. 38 GG. *Der Staat, 46*(3), 395–419.
Goodin, R. E. (1996). Enfranchising the earth, and its alternatives. *Political Studies, 44*(5), 835–849. https://doi.org/10.1111/j.1467-9248.1996.tb00337.x
Goodin, R. E. (2007). Enfranchising all affected interests, and its alternatives. *Philosophy & Public Affairs, 35*(1), 40–68. https://doi.org/10.1111/j.1088-4963.2007.00098.x
Habermas, J. (1993). *Justification and application: Remarks on discourse ethics.* MIT Press.
Habermas, J. (1998). *Between facts and norms: Contributions to a discourse theory of law and democracy.* (2nd Edition ed.; Trans., W. Rehg.) MIT Press.
Hammarberg, T. (2011). *Persons with Disabilities Must Not Be Denied the Right to Vote.* Accessed Retrieved 21. 21, 2019 September 2019, from https://www.coe.int/en/web/commissioner/-/persons-with-disabilities-must-not-be-denied-the-right-to-vo-2
Haraway, D. (1988). Situated knowledges: The science question in feminism and the privilege of partial perspective. *Feminist Studies, 14*(3), 575–599. https://doi.org/10.2307/3178066
Haslanger, S. A. (2013). *Resisting reality: Social construction and social critique.* Oxford University Press.
López-Guerra, C. (2012). Enfranchising minors and the mentally impaired. *Social Theory and Practice, 38*(1), 115–138. https://doi.org/10.5840/soctheorpract20123815
López-Guerra, C. (2014). *Democracy and disenfranchisement: The morality of electoral exclusions.* Oxford University Press.

Mráz, A. (2020). Disenfranchisement and the capacity/equality puzzle: Why disenfranchise children but not adults living with cognitive disabilities. *Moral Philosophy and Politics*, *7*(2), 255–279. https://doi.org/10.1515/mopp-2019-0054
Nussbaum, M. (2009). *Frontiers of justice. disability, nationality, species membership*. Harvard University Press.
Nussbaum, M. (2010). The capabilities of people with cognitive disabilities. In E. F. Kittay & L. Carlson (Eds.), *Cognitive disability and its challenge to moral philosophy* (pp. 75–95). Wiley-Blackwell.
Palleit, L. (2013). Zur Handlungsfähigkeit behinderter Menschen im Bereich politischer Grundrechte – Gleiches Recht auf Mitwirkung an Wahlen: Artikel 12 der UN-Behindertenrechtskonvention. In V. Aichele (Ed.), *Das Menschenrecht auf gleiche Anerkennung vor dem Recht* (pp. 302–326). Nomos.
Phillips, A. (1998). *The politics of presence: The political representation of gender, ethnicity, and race*. Clarendon Press.
Raad, R., Karlawish, J., & Appelbaum, P. S. (2009). The capacity to vote of persons with serious mental illness. *Psychiatric Services*, *60*(5), 624–628. https://doi.org/10.1176/ps.2009.60.5.624
Redley, M. (2008). Citizen with learning disabilities and the right to vote. *Disability & Society*, *23*(4), 375–384. https://doi.org/10.1080/09687590802038894
Scheffler, S. (2003). What is egalitarianism? *Philosophy & Public Affairs*, *31*(1), 5–39. https://doi.org/10.1111/j.1088-4963.2003.00005.x
Schemmel, C. (2015). Social equality - or just justice? In C. Fourie, F. Schuppert, & I. Wallimann-Helmer (Eds.), *Social equality - on what it means to be equals* (pp. 146–166). Oxford University Press.
Schramme, T. (2021). *Capable Deliberators: Towards Inclusion of Minority Minds in Discourse Practices*. Critical Review of International Social and Political Philosophy, Richard Bellamy. https://doi.org/10.1080/13698230.2021.2020550
Schriner, K., Ochs, L. A., & Shields, T. G. (1997). The last suffrage movement: voting rights for persons with cognitive and emotional disabilities. *Publius: The Journal of Federalism*, *27*(3), 75–96. https://doi.org/10.1093/oxfordjournals.pubjof.a029929
Schulte, B. (2012). Die UN-Behindertenrechtskonvention und der Ausschluss von Menschen mit Behinderungen vom Wahlrecht. *Zeitschrift für Rechtspolitik*, *45*(1), 16–18.
Sen, A. (2005). Human Rights and Capabilities. *Journal of Human Development*, *6*(2), 151–166. https://doi.org/10.1080/14649880500120491
Silvers, A. (1998). Formal Justice. In A. Silvers, D. Wasserman, & M. B. Mahowald (Eds.), *Disability, difference, discrimination: perspectives on justice in bioethics and public policy* (pp. 12–145). Rowman & Littlefield.
Waldron, J. (2012). *Dignity, rank, and rights* (M. Dan-Cohen, Ed.). Oxford University Press.
Waldschmidt, A. (2017). Disability goes cultural: the cultural model of disability as an analytical tool. In A. Waldschmidt, H. Berressem, & M. Ingwersen (Eds.), *Culture – theory – disability: encounters between disability studies and cultural studies* (pp. 19–27). Transcript.
Wasserman, D., Asch, A., Blustein, J., & Putnam, D. (2016). Disability: Definitions, models, experience. In E. N. Zalta (Ed.), *The stanford encyclopedia of philosophy*.
Young, I. M. (2004). *Inclusion and democracy*. Oxford University Press.
Young, I. M. (2011). *Justice and the politics of difference*. Princeton University Press.

Should refugees in the European Union have voting rights?

Ali Emre Benli

ABSTRACT
Most refugees residing in the European Union (EU) do not retain their voting rights in states of origin or lack the means to exercise them effectively. Most member states of the EU do not extend voting rights to refugees. This leaves a large population of refugees residing within the borders of the EU in a unique state of disenfranchisement. In this article, I consider this problem from a democratic perspective. Should refugees in the EU have voting rights? My answer turns on three aspects characterizing the circumstances of refugees: First, refugees reside in member states for an indeterminate, and typically protracted, amount of time without any exit options. Second, the political governance of the EU and its member states significantly shapes the lives of refugees. And third, refugees lack effective voting rights, and consequently, a meaningful political membership, in any political community across the world. In turn, based on an *all-subjected* principle of democratic inclusion, I argue that refugees should be secured state-level voting rights in member states, albeit with a condition of the period of residency. Moreover, they should have immediate voting rights at the supranational institutions of the EU such as the European Parliament.

Introduction

Most refugees residing in the European Union (EU) do not retain their voting rights in states of origin or lack the means to exercise them effectively. Most member states of the EU do not extend voting rights to refugees. This leaves more than 3 million refugees projected to reside within the borders of the EU in 2022 in a unique state of political disenfranchisement.[1] In this article, I wish to consider this problem from a democratic perspective. Should refugees in the EU have voting rights?

In Section 2, I begin by offering an overview of the voting rights of refugees residing in the EU in comparison to other non-citizen residents. The distinction is useful to illustrate refugees' distinct claim for voting rights in member states. In Section 3, I show that there are compelling reasons, grounded on an ideal of democratic inclusion, for securing voting rights for all individuals who are subjected to the governance of a political community. In Section 4, I demonstrate that refugees are subjected to the political governance of the member states in which they reside and have a claim to voting rights. In order for the member states to obtain democratic legitimacy, then, refugees should be enfranchised. Yet, there are also democratic concerns that caution against an unchecked expansion of the *demos*. In Section 5, I critically examine two of these concerns: First, that individuals who participate in democratic decision-making should be in a relationship of solidarity and trust. Second, that they should have an adequate knowledge of the language and the political culture of the political community. I find that these are reasonable concerns. Yet, none of them justify the current lack of refugees' voting rights in the EU. Alternatively, the two concerns should be addressed by institutions and policies designed to this end. In turn, I conclude that refugees' state-level voting rights must be secured in member states, albeit with a qualification on the period of residency. This is, nevertheless, a partial remedy. In turn, in Section 6, I make a further case for securing refugees *immediate* voting rights at the supranational institutions of the EU such as the European Parliament. Refugees' supranational voting rights would both give democratic legitimacy to the political governance of the EU and complement the qualified state-level voting rights in member states. Section 7 concludes.

Refugees' disenfranchisement is certainly not endemic to the EU. While the number of refugees is persistently increasing across the world,[2] most are devoid of access to meaningful voting rights (UN High Commissioner for Refugees (UNHCR), 2003; Hathaway, 2005, pp. 874–913). Yet, the issue has not gained much scholarly attention. Contemporary debates on refugee rights predominantly focus on social and economic rights as well as the rights concerning admission and stay in host territories (Gibney, 2004; Carens, 2013, pp. 192–225; Miller, 2017, pp. 76–94; Betts & Collier, 2017; Owen, 2013, 2019, 2020). The literature on the political rights of non-citizen residents does not sufficiently distinguish the circumstances of refugees (Beckman, 2006, pp. 153–165; Bauböck, 2007, pp. 2393–2448; Song, 2009, pp. 607–620). Recently, a number of commentaries have indeed discussed the political rights of refugees from democratic (Bender, 2021; Kapelner, 2020; Ziegler, 2017) as well as human rights (Ziegler, 2017) perspectives. This article joins these authors by addressing the question of refugees' voting rights in host member states. Yet, it is distinct in a number of ways: First, I identify stronger democratic grounds for refugees' voting rights in host communities by emphasizing the normative relevance of refugees' lack of effective voting rights, and in turn, their lack of meaningful political membership, in any state across the world from a democratic perspective. Second, notwithstanding the stronger democratic claim, I take democratic concerns that qualify enfranchisement as central to the normative analysis of voting rights. Hence, I argue that proposals for extending *immediate* voting rights to refugees at state level governance, such as the one advanced by Felix Bender (2021), are *unwarranted*. Finally, I make the case that the proper institutional setting for immediate voting rights is at the supranational level, as exemplified by the case of refugees residing in the EU. While the analysis I offer here is contextual, the arguments may be employed for refugees residing in other political communities with similar circumstances. It may also be employed for the design and implementation of supranational institutions other than those that can be found in the EU.

Voting rights of refugees residing in the EU

Refugees flee their states of origin and seek asylum in other states. A complete understanding of the political predicament of refugees in the EU requires, then, examining their voting rights in both host member states in which they reside, and the states of origin that they have fled. As I aim to show in this section, most refugees lack effective voting rights in both locations, leaving them in a distinct state of political disenfranchisement.

Let me begin with the first location. Across the EU, with respect to voting rights, refugees are treated as third country nationals. In other words, they have the same formal rights as other non-citizen residents who are not citizens of the EU. Refugees do not have the right to vote in national or European Parliament elections. More than half of the member states hold back from refugees the right to vote in local elections. In the remaining member states, refugees must legally reside in a member state for a period of 3 to 5 years before they acquire the right to vote in local elections.[3]

A way refugees may overcome their disenfranchisement in host member states is by becoming citizens through naturalization. Indeed, the 1951 *Refugee Convention* (Convention) recommends host states to facilitate refugees' naturalization (UN High Commissioner for Refugees (UNHCR), 2011). This is highly important, as citizenship implies full political enfranchisement. Yet there are also problems. First, at the level of international law, the Convention's recommendation is not formulated as a strong obligation (Hathaway, 2005, p. 981). Second, and perhaps more importantly, there is no institution that specifies the terms of naturalization. Each member state employs lengthy and demanding naturalization processes in accordance with their broader citizenship policies. These include requirements for language, residency and behavior, civic tests, monetary costs or allegiance oaths (Orgad, 2017; Weil, 2001). It is true that some states have eased up some requirements of naturalization for refugees in comparison with other migrants (Owen, 2019). For example, the requirement of residence is significantly reduced. Moreover, as David Owen notes, there is a general agreement among member states that renouncing the citizenship of the country of origin should not be relevant for refugees (Owen, 2019, pp. 350–352). Still, most refugees do not have the means to complete these processes; or they are not willing to naturalize under the morally contestable conditions determined by host states. Ultimately, large numbers of refugees remain for a protracted amount of time without voting rights across member states.[4]

What about refugee's voting rights in their state of origin? The answer may differ in relation to the definition of a refugee that one employs.[5] In accordance with the definition laid out by the Convention, a refugee is someone who is individually persecuted for reasons of race, religion, nationality, membership of a particular social group or political opinion (UN High Commissioner for Refugees (UNHCR), 2011). In some cases, the persecuted individuals are formally deprived of their voting rights by the persecuting state. In others, they retain formal voting rights; nevertheless, lack any meaningful access to exercise them.[6] For example, in cases where a refugee is under threat of persecution by the state of origin, even if she still has the right to vote, it may be that actual voting needs to be carried out in embassies, where the refugee may be exposed to the threat of persecution.

Alternatively, the definition of a refugee employed by the United Nations High Commissioner for Refugees (UNHCR) is broader. It comprises all those who are fleeing 'feared persecution, conflict, violence, or other circumstances that have seriously disturbed public order' (UN High Commissioner for Refugees (UNHCR), 2018, p. 1). In cases other than individual persecution, refugees may still have formal voting rights in their state of origin as well as the means to exercise them. Yet, exercising voting rights in a state of violence and conflict would not amount to a *meaningful influence* in the decision-making mechanisms of a political community, as such circumstances challenge the core of what defines a political community. It is true that some refugees are secured the right to vote in post-conflict scenarios, especially during peace-building processes. Yet, most conflicts are prolonged over long periods of time. In the handful of cases where post-conflict actors encourage mass political participation for shaping the emerging political community, refugees' inclusion faces serious obstacles (Ellis et al., 2007).

The lack of meaningful voting rights in states of origin signifies, for both the Convention and the UNHCR definitions of a refugee, that refugees lack a meaningful political membership in states of origin. In beginning of the section, I noted that refugees in the EU, in terms of voting rights, are treated as third country nationals. Yet, their lack of meaningful voting rights, and in turn, a meaningful political membership in states of origin, distinguishes them from many other groups of non-citizen residents in the EU. In the following, I try to clarify this distinction, which is useful to illuminate refugees' specific democratic claim for voting rights in member states, by commenting on two possible objections. Note, nevertheless, that by making this distinction, I do not wish to argue that other groups of non-citizen residents should not have voting rights in member states. My aim, instead, is to specify the circumstances of refugees that grounds the specific argument for voting rights I develop in Section 4.

First, one may point out that many immigrants residing in member states do not have external voting rights. Hence, one may argue that immigrants who fall into this category do not have meaningful access to voting rights in states of origin as well. If this is the case, the distinction I wish to make between refugees and third country nationals is not as stark as I depict it to be. The descriptive point of the objection is plausible. Not all states ensure external voting for expatriates (Ellis et al., 2007). Accordingly, many immigrants residing in member states do not have the means to exercise their right to vote in elections of their states of origin. This may be, for example, due to the simple fact that travelling to states of origin is too costly. Yet, it would be misleading to maintain, based on this point, that the immigrants who do not have the means to cast their vote in states of origin are in a similar situation as refugees. The lack of external voting rights may constitute a problem of political representation for expatriates. Moreover, there may be democratic arguments for ensuring expatriate rights. Yet, the latter are not disenfranchised in the way that refugees are. This is because refugees' lack of effective voting rights in states of origin is due to their circumstances qua being refugees: In some cases, refugees have no legal rights vote in home country elections. In cases where they retain their right to vote, refugees do not have the right to return to host states while keeping their refugee status. Finally, if refugees travel to home states in irregular ways, they are under the threat of persecution.

Second, one may further point out that not all states that include external voting for expatriates in their elections are democratic states. Similar to the first point, one may then argue that immigrants who fall into this category do not have a meaningful influence in the decision-making mechanisms of their state of origin as well. The descriptive point of this objection is also plausible. Upon consideration, it may turn out that political governance in many states of origin do not meet the democratic standards that member states of the EU uphold. Yet, it would again be misleading, based on this fact, to assert that immigrants belonging to this group are in a similar situation as refugees. Earlier, I have suggested that, in some contexts such as an ongoing civil war, refugees' formal voting rights do not amount to a *meaningful influence* in political governance. This claim is indeed about the characteristics of governance in the political community that refugees are to exercise their voting rights. Admittedly, the characteristics of a political community that ensures a *meaningful influence* for its members, and in turn, a meaningful political membership, is here underspecified. Such a specification, moreover, is beyond the scope of the argument I wish to develop here. Nevertheless, we should be wary of inflating the idea of a *meaningful influence* through demanding criteria of democratic self-government. As long as political governance provides its citizens a set of basic rights, and at the same time, ensures some mechanisms of participation and accountability in its decision-making mechanisms, we may assume that voting constitutes meaningful influence.

Democratic grounds of voting rights

Refugees residing in the EU, then, have no access to meaningful voting rights in any political community across the world. In Section 4, I argue that the particular disenfranchisement of refugees plays a crucial role in developing refugees' distinct claim for voting rights in member states. Before doing that, in this section, my aim is to specify the *normative reasons* that may ground this claim.

In a recent article, Bender (2021) argues, based on an *all-subjected* principle of democratic inclusion, that all refugees should be enfranchised in liberal democratic states.[7] In turn, he claims that all refugees should be extended *immediate* state-level voting. How plausible is Bender's claim? The relevance of the *all-subjected* principle for the circumstances of refugees in the EU, and its diverging implications for state and supranational levels of governance will be of concern in the subsequent sections. Here, the prior question I take up is: how plausible is an *all-subjected* principle of democratic inclusion for grounding voting rights?

The question is placed within a debate on what has come to be called the *democratic boundary problem*. The debate initiates from the recognition that for a political community to obtain democratic legitimacy, not only its decision-making processes should be assessed by an ideal of democracy but also the constitution of its *demos*, that is, the group of individuals who have a right to partake in its decision-making processes. At the core of an ideal of democracy, as Arash Abizadeh puts, is 'a vision of human beings as inherently *free* and *equal*' (Abizadeh, 2008, p. 39). According to democrats like Abizadeh, in contemporary political communities, where individuals are governed through binding laws and regulations, this vision can only be achieved with reference to an ideal of *collective self-governance* where all see themselves as not only the subjects but also the authors of these laws and regulations. Individual autonomy, in other words, can only be sustained by public autonomy (Abizadeh, 2008, pp. 38–42). Yet, it is also a characteristic of contemporary political communities that the link that ties one individual to a specific political governance is often blurred. For example, many laws and regulations of a political governance impact those who live outside its jurisdiction. Many individuals regularly cross borders to reside within the territories of political communities in which they are not formal members. In order to conceptualize an ideal of collective self-governance, then, we need to ask: Which specific relationship between an individual and a political governance triggers the claim to be included in decision-making processes? This is one way to formulate the main question that motivates the democratic boundary problem.

In an extensive literature, theorists offer at least two types of principles, each recognizing a different relationship as the normatively relevant one for constituting the *demos*. The *all-subjected* principle is one type of principle. It holds that what grounds the democratic claim to inclusion is *subjection to political governance*.[8] Other theorists emphasize the *presence of affected interest* as grounding democratic inclusion.[9] Here I wish to side-step a discussion of the relative merits of the two types of principle, and explore, similar to Bender, an *all-subjected* principle for considering the grounds of refugee's voting rights. One reason is that, as I will aim to show, the *all-subjected* principle is well placed to capture the specific demand of inclusion in voting processes.[10] But the other is pragmatic. The *all-subjected* principle is significantly more demanding than the principle of *all-affected interests*. If refugees are subjected to the political governance of a member state, then, it follows that their interests are also affected in significant ways by the outcomes of decision-making in member states. In other words, if it can be shown that refugees have a democratic claim for a right to vote, based on an *all-subjected* principle, then, the same reasons would suffice to ground voting rights by an *all-affected-interest* principle.

Let's take a closer look, then, to the *all-subjected* principle for democratic inclusion. What does it mean to be subjected to a political governance? In the recent literature, we find two senses of *being subjected* to a political governance: one regards being subjected to the *coercive power* of laws and regulations, and the other, *being governed* by a political authority. The first sense, prominently formulated by Arash Abizadeh (2008), emphasizes the autonomy infringing character of coercive acts and coercive threats of a state in enforcing its laws and regulations. In order for such infringement of autonomy to be legitimized, Abizadeh argues, coercive laws and regulations should be designed and implemented through democratic processes that all who are subjected to them should take part (Abizadeh, 2008, p. 40). In the second sense, *being governed* by a political authority is more demanding. It is conditional upon being subjected to a set of *life-shaping* laws and regulations (Miller, 2020). These can be formulated as grounds rules that govern social interactions (Fraser, 2008, p. 411) or *regulate* autonomy, rather than mere instances of autonomy infringement (Bender, 2021).

The two senses of subjection, in the first instance, seem to point at distinct normative concerns, and possibly, to different conclusions with regards to claims of inclusion. Yet, they may also be interpreted as versions of the same principle that take up different roles. The difference arises due to what democratic inclusion implies, namely, that all individuals *bind themselves*, through collective processes of authorization, as both subjects and authors of the laws and regulations that they are subjected to.[11] The first sense, as Abizadeh emphasizes, provides a standard of critique that reveals where a demand for democratic legitimization arises (Abizadeh, 2008, p. 56). For democratic legitimacy, any exercise of coercion by states should be legitimized. Yet not all types of coercion demand similar processes of collective authorization. For example, the voting rights I raise here regards refugees' inclusion as *equal participants* in state and supranational level elections.[12] Equal participation in state or supra-national level elections, moreover, demands individuals to bind themselves in comprehensive ways. This is because these institutions govern nearly all aspects of individuals public life. For equal participation in such a demanding process of collective authorization to be initiated, mere instances coercion is not sufficient. Instead, the democratic claim for voting rights is better captured by the sense of subjection as *being governed* by a political authority.

Should refugees have voting rights in member states?

An *all-subjected* principle of democratic inclusion in the sense described above may then ground a claim to voting rights. Yet are refugees subjected to the governance of member states? At least three features of refugees' circumstances in member states may lead us to conclude that they do so: (a) the extent and scope of the rules and regulations that they are subject to, (b) the protracted and indeterminate period of stay without exit options, and (c) the lack of a meaningful political membership in states of origin. In what follows, I briefly discuss each feature, and show how they place refugees residing in member states within the scope of the *all-subjected* principle.

(a) *Political governance of member states significantly shapes the lives of refugees.*

Political institutions of the member states govern the lives of refugees at two levels. At one level, refugees are subjected to political governance as other non-citizens residing within member state territory. Such governance includes laws and regulations that organize daily life or policies that shape the opportunities and expectation of all residents. At another level, refugees are governed *qua* being refugees. The member states of the EU are signatories to the Convention as well as international human rights treaties that set minimal standards for states' treatment of refugees and other residents within their territory. These include basic rights to family, work, education, healthcare and so on. Yet, the implementation of these rights depends on state-level policies. For example, some refugees have a hard time having access to work or education in member states, others are hosted in refugee camps in dire living conditions. Moreover, state-level policies regulate processes that determine refugees' legal status. Again, these standards are provided by international treaties. Their implementation is overseen by the UNHCR. Yet here also state-level policy making matters. For example, some member states employ fast-track status determination procedures without any meaningful judicial appeal opportunities for refugees, leading to unjustified cases of repatriation.

(b) *Refugees reside in member states for an indeterminate, and typically protracted, amount of time without any exit options.*

The nature of refugees' period of stay in member states can be explained with reference to the international refugee regime and the current state of refugee governance across the world. Refugees have an internationally recognized legal right to remain in member states unless a long-term solution to their refugeehood is found. Grounded on a principle of *non-refoulement*, member states cannot deport refugees to a state where their lives or liberties would be in danger or states where the principle of *non-refoulement* may not be respected (UN High Commissioner for Refugees (UNHCR), 2011, p. 30). Yet, as Owen cautions, 'the right to remain is not a right to permanent residence but rather a right to reside for whatever period is required to secure protection' (Owen, 2018, pp. 333–334). Long term solutions for refugees' predicament are, nevertheless, scarce. Refugees can be resettled to a third country that volunteers to take full responsibility. Or they can be repatriated to their states of origin, if the reasons for refugeehood are resolved. In reality, the number of refugees resettled are extremely low. Conditions in states of origin that lead to refugeehood, such as persecution or conflict, are usually protracted.[13] Moreover, as Zeigler notes, neither 'refugees nor their states of asylum know *when* or, indeed, *whether* such changes in circumstances will occur' (Ziegler, 2017, p. 198). In other words, refugees' period of stay in member states is *indeterminate*. The most likely prospect for them is to remain in member states until they are eligible for naturalization. Finally, within this international framework, refugees have no *exit options* (Bender, 2021, p. 2; Ziegler, 2017, p. 198). They may not return to the state of origin. Moreover, they may not move to other states, unless through resettlement, due to policies that regulate the distribution of responsibility among a group of states, such as the *first country of arrival rule* employed in the EU; or the *third safe country rule*, based on which states justify sending asylum seekers back to a *safe state* that they were present before entering their territory (Hathaway, 2005, pp. 293–297). Of course, beyond these practices, any state has the right to take the responsibility of an asylum claimant within its territory. But such cases happen rarely and cannot be considered as a *real exit option* for refugees residing in host states.

The outlined conditions of refugees' period of residence in member states enhance the *life-shaping* character of both levels of governance discussed in (a). The protracted period of stay significantly augments the impact of the rules and regulations that refugees are subjected to. Moreover, considering the indeterminacy of the period of stay together with the lack of exit options, it is reasonable to expect refugees to develop their life-plans as residents who are there to stay, given the opportunity to become members of the political community in which they reside. In turn, refugees are agents suitable for *binding* processes of collective authorization such as state-level elections. Importantly, these circumstances distinguish refugees from transients, such as tourists or short-term residents, who may be subjected to the coercive laws and regulations of member states but do not fall under the scope of the *all-subjected* principle. But they also distinguish refugees from those long-term residents who have *exit options*. The latter group, unless shown otherwise, cannot immediately be considered as agents that bind themselves by the outcomes of processes of collective authorization as refugees.

(c) *Refugees lack meaningful political membership in states of origin.*

I have discussed the ways in which refugees are disenfranchised in both states of origin and member states in Section 2. The lack of voting rights in states of origin, moreover, signifies a lack of meaningful political membership in states of origin. Yet why should refugees' political circumstances in states of origin matter for a claim regarding their political subjection in host states? The point is perhaps clearer when we look at the political subjection of other forms of non-citizen residents in member states who retain a meaningful political membership in states of origin. As I aim to show in the following, unlike many other non-citizen residents for whom significant domains of life are shaped by the governance of states of origin, all domains of refugees' lives are subjected to the governance of host states.

First, although non-citizen residents in member states do not reside within the territories of states of origin, they are still *directly* subjected to their rules and regulations in a number of domains. These range from laws that govern the terms of marriage or inheritance to policies regarding taxation and property rights. Second, in a number of cases, states of origin have an *indirect* influence, through bilateral agreements, over the regulations which non-citizen residents are subject to in member states. One example is the agreement between Turkey and Germany concerning the organization of the lives of Turkish citizens residing in Germany. This includes, for example, organization of places of worship as well as training of religious leaders. But more generally, any state of origin may take responsibility for its citizens residing in other states in cases of maltreatment. Finally, states of origin take part in *international processes* that shape a significant part of the ground rules that have *life-shaping* implications for all individuals across the world. These range from rights conventions to treatise regarding international trade, environment and climate change or the use of nuclear power. Refugees, on the other hand, lack a meaningful political membership in states of origin that can take a role in any of these domains. The scope of home state governance, at both levels discussed in (a), is in turn broader for refugees in comparison with many other forms of non-citizens residents. The *life-shaping* character of home states' rule and regulations is again enhanced.

If the distinctions offered here are plausible, then refugees are subjected to the political governance in member states in significant ways. The circumstances of refugees in host states as well as states of origin place them within the scope of the *all-subjected* principle. Refugees residing in member states, then, have a democratic claim for voting rights that is stronger than what Ziegler and Bender anticipates.[14] Yet how should this normative claim be met in practice? Which rights must be secured for refugees residing in member states?

Democratic reasons for curtailing voting rights

Recall that the aim of this investigation is to consider the question of refugees' voting rights in member states from a democratic perspective. In turn, the task of determining the specific voting rights that must be secured for refugees need to take into account other democratic considerations. Accordingly, in this section, I consider two views that caution against extending the right to vote in a way that undermines democratic processes. If these concerns apply for the case of refugees residing in member states, then, the voting rights of refugees may be curtailed for democratic reasons.

The first view concerns the relationship between individuals who engage in collective practices of authorization. David Miller, among others, argues that individuals should be in a relationship of solidarity and trust in order to recognize the outcomes of democratic processes as legitimate (2009, p. 206; 2017, p. 644; Bellamy, 2020, pp. 43–44, 79). Solidarity and trust, Miller further claims, obtains among those who share a national identity, characterized by a shared culture, language and history (Miller, 2017, pp. 144–145). The second view concerns the *properties* of individuals. According to Will Kymlicka, for democratic processes to deliver legitimate outcomes, individuals need to have an adequate knowledge of the language and political culture of the political community. A common language is necessary, for, as Kymlicka puts it, 'democratic politics is politics in the vernacular' (Kymlicka, 2001, p. 213). Knowledge of the political culture is necessary for individuals to understand the political system as well as the political questions that have historically occupied the community (Miller, 2017, pp. 130–151; Bellamy, 2020, pp. 43–44,

79). Richard Bellamy calls these conditions the *polity aspects* of a political governance (Bellamy, 2020, p. 65). From a democratic perspective, Bellamy argues, the polity aspects ensure a sense of identification that motivates individuals to consider collectively binding decisions as both 'legitimate and plausible' (Bellamy, 2020, p. 46).

According to these views, then, state-level voting should be extended to individuals only if they are in the relevant relations with each other and possess the required properties. Most refugees, nevertheless, are not nationals of the member states in which they reside. Most of them do not have the knowledge of the political culture. The solution, for Miller, is naturalization processes designed to 'nationalize' newcomers. As any other non-national resident, then, the voting rights of refugees should not be secured until and unless they are naturalized. Yet, this proves to be a major obstacle for refugees' voting rights in member states. For, as I discuss in Section 2, in practice, naturalization processes leave out a significant number of refugees from access to citizenship, and in turn, to voting rights.

Let's take a step back and ask how plausible are these concerns? It is reasonable to maintain that democratic processes would lose their character as a collective practice of authorization, unless individuals are motivated to find common grounds and trust each other for their reasons and criticism to be sincere, rather than exploiting the processes to bring about their own interests. Yet, this does not immediately commit us to follow Miller in a demand for naturalization. For it is not clear what constitutes solidarity and trust among individuals. Even if national identity may play an important role in many contemporary societies, there may be alternatives such as a shared commitment to democratic principles or pursuing joint activities (Sevinç, 2019). Equally unclear is the degree of knowledge of the language and political culture of the political community that individuals should possess in order for the democratic processes to function well. For Kymlicka, such knowledge is not only technical but also has a ritualistic component without which individuals may not be able to understand democratic debates. Yet, others point out that the ritualistic elements are extremely diverse for all to be comprehended by each individual (Weinstock, 2001, pp. 55–62). Some knowledge of a common language devoted to political communication, moreover, may suffice to ensure the quality of processes as long as individuals are willing to engage with each other in democratic ways (Archibugi, 2008, pp. 249–274). The level of shared knowledge, then, need not be too advanced.

Many argue, moreover, that political communities may mediate the requirements of democratic processes by institutional design (Pevnick, 2009, pp. 148–150; Shachar, 2009, pp. 148–152). For example, policies may be implemented towards creating inclusive shared identities and community building. These may aim to increase the level and the quality of social interactions among citizens and refugees. Accessible educational programmes may be created for newcomers. Financial resources may be extended to refugees for enabling them to attend such programmes. Given the challenges of the problem with respect to its unique characteristics, an all-fitting solution cannot be formulated. Instead, the matter may only be settled individually for each member state of the EU. Yet, note that the requirements of democratic inclusion delineated in the previous sections places stringent duties on host states: if states aim to sustain democratic legitimacy, they need to secure refugees' meaningful paths of democratic participation irrespective of the condition of naturalization. If there are feasible and accessible institutions that can meet the democratic concerns, then, states have duties to implement them together with the voting rights of refugees.

What does this imply for the case of refugee's voting rights in member states? Let's assume, for the sake of the argument, that member states may sustain the democratic concerns raised by Miller, Kymlicka and Bellamy by a set of institutions design to this end. Do we have a case for securing *immediate* state level voting rights for refugees? Not necessarily. For there remains a necessary condition for their fulfillment shared by all on both sides of the debate. In order to enjoy some level of solidarity and trust as well as to possess some shared sense of the political culture, individuals need to develop social relationships with at least some part of the political community. This is so even under the most suitable institutional arrangements. The development of social relationships, moreover, needs time as well as a shared space in which individuals engage in social interactions. Most refugees who have recently arrived in host states have not shared a social space with other residents.[15] In practice, the heuristic is the time. Not all refugees have resided in host states for an adequate amount of time to meet the democratic concerns. It is reasonable to assert, then, that refugees' state-level voting rights can only be secured after a period of residence. The proposals for refugees' immediate voting rights advanced by authors such as Bender (2021), then, remain *unwarranted*. Refugees residing in member states should have the right to vote at state level elections, albeit with a qualification based on the period of residency.

What should be the period of residence required for securing refugees' state-level voting rights in member states? Ziegler, for example, cites New Zealand as implementing the best practice where the permanent-residence status acquired after legal recognition of refugee status secures refugees state-level voting rights within a one-year period. An important assumption motivating this proposal is that state's commitment to extend state-level voting rights in such a short time would motivate refugees to establish social relationship and acquire the relevant properties to engage in democratic processes. As Ziegler notes, nevertheless, the feasibility of the policy essentially depends on the particular social, political and geographical circumstances of New Zealand (Ziegler, 2017, pp. 218–220). A comparative assessment of New Zealand and the EU member states is beyond the scope of this article. Yet, one may reasonably suggest that, for the latter, such favorable conditions do not sufficiently obtain to secure refugees' voting rights within one year. Alternatively, Owen, among others, argues for placing the residency requirement of naturalization to three-years (Owen, 2013, pp. - 333–334, 2019, pp. 348–350; Price, 2009). Given institutions designed to this end, three years may indeed turn out to be a feasible amount of time for resolving the democratic concerns. If widely implemented across member states, moreover, fast-tracking naturalization would diminish the scale of refugees' political disenfranchisement, as the number of individuals lacking political rights would significantly decrease.

Yet, this is a partial remedy. On the one hand, the naturalization requirements that remain would still constitute a significant barrier for refugees' access to citizenship, and in turn, to voting rights. On the other hand, there would continue to be a large number of refugees without voting rights in the 3-year period. In the next section, I develop a proposal that *complements* state-level voting rights: refugees residing in member states should have *immediate* voting rights in the supranational decision-making mechanisms of the EU. As I will argue, supranational voting rights would not only meet the demands of democratic legitimacy that emerge in virtue of supranational institutions of governance but also alleviate the democratic shortcomings of the condition of residence attached to state-level voting.

Voting rights of refugees in the EU

Should refugees have voting rights in the governing institutions of the EU? In addressing this question, I consider whether the conditions that ground refugees' state-level voting rights also ground their voting rights at the EU level. But before doing that, let me begin by asking whether the supranational level decision-making mechanisms of the EU constitutes a distinct level of governance that calls for its own investigation of democratic inclusion? In other words, are there in fact two separate questions that can not be reduced to each other: one concerning inclusion in the supranational demos, and another, in the national demo constituting it?

Rainer Bauböck argues that the democratic legitimacy of supranational institutions cannot solely be derived from the democratic legitimacy of the states constituting it. This is because decisions taken by intergovernmental mechanisms are not always endorsed by the citizens of the union of states as a whole. In order to remedy this mismatch, supranational institutions should derive democratic legitimacy from a supranational demos (Bauböck, 2018, pp. 62–63). Yet, who should be included in a supranational *demos*? For

Bauböck, the *demos* of the EU should be constituted by EU citizens. EU citizenship, moreover, should be derivative of member state citizenship. In other words, supranational voting rights should be reserved for the citizens of the states constituting the union.

Bauböck bases this claim on the observation that the grounds of being a citizen of a union of states are not universal but historical and geographical (Bauböck, 2018, pp. 80–87). This is plausible. EU citizenship serves the needs of the EU integration project by granting member state citizens a whole bundle of rights, including freedom of movement and consular protection. Other unions of states may have different integration aims and grant its union citizens those rights that specifically serve these aims. The grounds of supranational citizenship, then, include reasons arising from the specific context. These reasons, nevertheless, cannot wholly be accounted by a distinct principle of democratic inclusion at the suprastate level.

Note, nevertheless, that this argument applies at the state-level as well. The bundle of rights citizenship comprises of, as well as its acquisition requirements, differ from one state to another. First, citizenship entails more than voting rights. For example, it secures individuals an extensive set of socio-economic rights, ensures a definitive right to stay and grants immediate citizenship to those newborns to citizens. Second, similar to supranational citizenship policies, state citizenship is designed to achieve particular economic, social and political ends. Therefore, in Bauböck's terms, not all grounds of state-citizenship are universal. Some are historical and geographical. Importantly, these reasons need not be democratic. It may refer to a genuine connection arising out of the social fact of membership (Shachar, 2009, pp. 164–193). It may be based on other moral grounds. For example, a state, based on a commitment not to render children stateless, may follow a policy of citizenship acquisition by descent (*jus sanguinis*) for its citizens who migrate to those states that have residence based (*jus soli*) citizenship acquisition policies. Or it may even implement citizenship policies in accordance with its economic and technological goals (Shachar & Hirschl, 2014).

What does this imply for the question at hand? As inclusion into the citizenry is not solely motivated by democratic concerns, citizenship cannot solely be grounded on *democratic* principles. Bluntly put, there is no principle of *democratic* inclusion that alone grounds the claims to citizenship. Instead, the democratic question regards the inclusion of individuals in processes of collective authorization. The grounds of voting should, then, be *disaggregated* from the grounds of citizenship. This does not mean that, in practice, the right to vote should be disaggregated from the right to citizenship. In some cases, disaggregation may have harmful consequences for democratic processes. For example, some object that the tight linkage between state-level voting and citizenship is an indispensable aspect of the nation-state (song, 2009, p. 607). Others caution against unintended consequences.

Disaggregation, they point out, is a slippery slope that may lead to a segregated society: there may emerge of a class of long-term residents without access to citizenship (Shachar, 2009, p. 223; Benhabib, 2004, p. 146). Both objections are plausible. Serious consideration should be given to the *implications* of institutional solutions that involve disaggregating voting rights from citizenship. Yet, this does not prevent us from distinguishing their distinct normative grounds when considering refugees' claim for voting rights.

We may then conclude, with Bauböck, that the supranational governance of the EU constitutes a domain with a distinct question of democratic inclusion. Yet, contrary to Bauböck, the question of voting rights at the supranational level need not be based solely on member state citizenship. Alternatively, as I argue in Section 3, the ground of voting rights is best captured by an *all-subjected* principle of democratic inclusion. The next step is to delineate whether refugees residing in the EU fall within the scope of the *all-subjected* principle.

Should refugees residing in the EU have voting rights in its supranational institution? Are refugees subjected to the political governance of the EU? Note that the two conditions ((b) and (c)) characterizing the circumstances of refugees residing in member states, discussed in Section 4, directly apply at the EU level: Refugees reside within the territory of the EU for an indeterminate, and typically protracted, amount of time without any exit options. Moreover, refugees lack meaningful political membership in states of origin. The issue then turns on whether the third condition (a) also applies: Does the political governance of the EU significantly shape the lives of refugees residing in member states?

Refugees are governed by the institutions of the EU at three levels. First, they are subjected to the laws and regulations of the EU as any other resident. These include the domains of social and economic interaction regulated by EU institutions. Second, refugees are subjected *qua* being refugees. In Section 4, I have emphasized the role of state-level policies in shaping the lives of refugees residing in member states. Nevertheless, EU level policy making also have significant implications. For example, although the refugee decision should be taken by a member state, it is guided by EU law. In addition, there are a series of EU institutions that provide the framework for refugee protection across Europe. For example, the Common European Asylum System aims to ensure equal standards of protections across member states and lays out the criteria for responsibility distribution. Institutions such as the Asylum, Migration and Integration Fund (AMIF) provide support to member states in the face of sudden arrivals of large numbers. Agencies such as European Dactyloscopy, the EU fingerprint database (EURODAC), and the European Border and Coast Guard Agency (FRONTEX) facilitate common administration of borders. Yet, perhaps the most comprehensive EU level governance is exemplified by the New Pact on Migration and Asylum, recently proposed by the European Commission, that aims to integrate migration policies across the EU.[16] At a third level, the institutions of the EU oversee member state activities. This is highly important in ensuring refugees' exercise of their rights *qua* refugees as well as securing their fundamental human rights in the absence of state-level voting rights. In cases of transgression from EU law, institutions such as the European Parliament or the European commission may hold member states accountable. Or refugees may take member states to the European Court of Human Rights.

Given the scope of the rules and regulations that govern the lives of refugees at these three levels, together with the conditions (b) and (c), we may maintain that refugees residing in member states are subjected to the political governance of the EU in *life-shaping* ways. In turn, refugees should be secured the right to vote in its supranational decision-making mechanisms, such as the European Parliament, grounded on an *all-subjected* principle of democratic inclusion.

Yet how would an institutional setting that secures refugees' rights to vote in the supranational institutions of the EU look like? An extensive treatment of this question is beyond the scope of this paper. Still, to give some content to the implications of the argument I develop here, let me briefly outline two mechanism that could be implemented within the European Parliament. One alternative is to secure all refugees residing in the EU, whose status is legally recognized, the right to vote in European Parliament elections. Considering the large number of refugees residing in the EU, projected to pass more than 3 million in 2022, the members of the European Parliament as well as European political parties would likely be responsive to the interests and demands of refugees. Refugees' right to vote may, then, be considered as an effective mechanism that enhances the democratic legitimacy of the EU. Another alternative is to secure refugees not only to the right to vote but also the right to stand in European Parliament elections. For example, refugees may be allocated seats in the European Parliament in accordance with the population of a *non-territorial* Refugee Community created within the territory of the EU. Securing refugees' right to vote together with the right to stand in elections in the European Parliament would likely to enhance more the democratic legitimacy of the EU in comparison with the first proposal. Yet, it would require additional institutional arrangements that require a greater political will for their implementation.

Before concluding, nevertheless, one final task remains. We need to consider whether the democratic views that caution against extending refugees the right to vote at state-level governance also applies at the supranational level. Should the supranational voting rights of refugees also be conditional upon a period of residency?

Not necessarily. The main reason is that the polity aspects associated with state-level governance is not as demanding at the EU level. In fact, as Bellamy observes, in the current state of the EU, 'Social and economic divergence, on the one side, and culture and linguistic diversity, on the other, remain robust' (Bellamy, 2020, p. 84). First, the level of solidarity and trust, based on interpersonal identification, that one may find among the citizens of member states does not obtain among the citizens of the EU. According to recent surveys, 'only 2% of EU citizens view themselves as "Europeans" pure and simple, with a mere 6% regarding a European identity as more important than their national one' (Bellamy 2020, p. 84). Second, it would be an overreach to claim that the EU has a common political culture. It is true that all member states are committed to the rights that figure in the European Convention of Human Rights and the EU Charter of Rights. Yet, as Bellamy notes, 'this does not mean that they should automatically believe it legitimate to deliberate about them as a common people' (Bellamy, 2020, p. 86). Each community, instead, brings into the democratic debate considerations and insights from diverse political cultures. Finally, multilingualism is one of the EU's founding principles. In the European Parliament, for example, the meetings are translated into all 24 official languages.

One may argue that these are aspects of EU level decision-making that are detrimental to democracy and should be remedied. This may be a reasonable ideal. Yet, it does not justify rendering refugees' EU level voting rights conditional upon the presence of polity aspects, at least in the current conditions characterizing the EU. For refugees' case for voting rights should not be assessed by criteria that does not obtain among citizens of the member states. Moreover, it is also reasonable to maintain that, given the greater extent and scope of decision-making at state-level governance in comparison with supranational governance, the polity aspects of the latter *need not* be as demanding, even under more robust democratic standards. Based on an *all-subjected* principle of democratic inclusion, refugees should then be secured *immediate* supranational voting rights.

Conclusion

Recent years have seen a significant increase in the number of refugees across the world. It is reasonable to assume, moreover, that this trend will continue. Specifically, within the EU, the number of individuals without voting rights has overtaken the population of some of its member states. The main motivation behind this article is to bring to the fore refugees' disenfranchisement in Europe. Refugees are a group of individuals who distinctively lack meaningful voting rights in any political community across the world. Moreover, their conditions *qua* being refugees compel them to reside in member states for an indeterminate, and typically protracted, amount of time without any exit options. From a democratic perspective, then, refugees' subjection to governance in member states should be legitimized by their inclusion in collective processes of authorization. The multi-level political governance of the EU creates a unique opportunity to meet this demand for democratic inclusion. If the arguments I offer here are plausible, refugees should have state-level voting rights after a period of residency. But they should also have *immediate* voting rights in the supranational institutions of governance of the EU such as the European Parliament.

Notes

1. See the projection by the United Nations High Commissioner for Refugees Global Appeal 2022. Accessible at: https://www.unhcr.org/globalappeal2022/.
2. According to the UNHCR, the number of refugees across the world have reached 26.4 million in 2020. Accessible at: https://www.unhcr.org/figures-at-a-glance.html.
3. The exception is Finland where the residence requirement is at least 2 years on the 51st day before the elections. For electoral rights in the EU, see https://globalcit.eu/conditions-for-electoral-rights/.
4. For example, as Ragab and Antara observes, despite the fact that Germany is a major host of refugees in the EU, between the years 2000 and 2015, merely 21,754 Syrian nationals has been naturalized into German citizenship (Ragab & Antara, 2018, p. 11).
5. There is an ongoing scholarly debate on conceptualizing refugeehood. While some defend the Convention definition (Cherem, 2016), others argue for broadening it to include those who flee human rights deprivations (Shacknove, 1985). Note that the issue of political disenfranchisement applies to both definitions.
6. See Ziegler's discussion of *de facto* disenfranchised refugees (Ziegler, 2017, pp. 133–159).
7. See also, Ziegler (2017) for a case for enfranchising refugees in states of asylum that draws upon a variety of normative and pragmatic considerations.
8. For various formulations of the principle, see, Benhabib (2004, p. 217), Lopez-Guerra (2005), Fraser (2008, pp. 407–413), Abizadeh (2008), Näsström (2011), and Owen (2012).
9. An *all-affected-interest* principle may be formulated as: all whose interests are affected by the outcome of a decision should be included in the decision-making processes. For alternative formulations, see, Arrhenius (2005), Goodin (2007), and Song (2009).
10. Alternatively, the *all-affected-interest* principle may ground claims for representation of interests. For a discussion of this view, see, Owen (2012) and Bauböck (2018).
11. See Erman (2014) for a discussion of the condition of bindingness. Also, Lopez-Guerra for the emphasis on *binding* legislative processes for an all-subjected principle (Lopez-Guerra, 2005, p. 224).
12. Here I am employing an illuminating distinction by Owen between 'an equal right of participation in the demos' and 'a right of equal participation in the demos' (Owen, 2012, p. 147).

13. For example, according to UNHCR, in 2019, while the number of refugees across the world reached 29 million, the number of returned refugees remained at 317,281. (https://www.unhcr.org/refugee-statistics/download/?url=JvW7).
14. While Ziegler (2017) and Bender (2021) discuss (a) and (b) as grounds of inclusion, they do not take into account (c).
15. Some refugees choose to seek asylum in political communities where they have already existing social ties. Yet, these cases are exceptions.
16. See New Pact on Migration and Asylum (available at: https://ec.europa.eu/info/strategy/priorities-2019-2024/promoting-our-european-way-life/new-pact-migration-and-asylum_en).

Acknowledgments

I am thankful for the feedback I received on earlier versions of this article from the audiences in Amsterdam, Braga, Edinburgh, Göttingen, Manchester, and Istanbul. For individual comments, I would like to thank Ayelet Shachar, Axel Gosseries, Benedikt Buechel, Benjamin Boudou, Eszter Kollar, Kieran Oberman, Marcus Carlsen Häggrot, Sebastian Rudas, Sine Bagatur and Tamar de Waal.

Disclosure statement

No potential conflict of interest was reported by the author(s).

ORCID

Ali Emre Benli http://orcid.org/0000-0002-0178-7779

References

Abizadeh, A. (2008). Democratic theory and border coercion: No right to unilaterally control your own borders. *Political Theory*, *36*(1), 37–65. https://doi.org/10.1177/0090591707310090

Archibugi, D. (2008). *The Global Commonwealth of Citizens: Towards Cosmopolitan Democracy*. Princeton University Press.

Arrhenius, G. (2005). The Boundary Problem in Democratic Theory. In F. Tersman (Ed.), *Democracy Unbound: Basic Explorations* (pp. 14–29). Filosofiska Institutionen.

Bauböck, R. (2007). Stakeholder Citizenship and Transnational Political Participation: A Normative Evaluation of External Voting. *Fordham Law Review*, *75*(5) , 2393–2448. https://ir.lawnet.fordham.edu/flr/vol75/iss5/4/

Bauböck, R. (2018). Democratic inclusion: A pluralist theory of citizenship. In D. Owen (Ed.), *Democratic Inclusion: Rainer Bauböck in Dialogue* (pp. 3–103). Manchester University Press.

Beckman, L. (2006). Citizenship and Voting Rights: Should Resident Aliens Vote? *Citizenship Studies*, *10*(2), 153–165. https://doi.org/10.1080/13621020600633093

Bellamy, R. (2020). *A Republican Europe of States. Cosmopolitanism, Intergovernmentalism and Democracy in the EU*. Cambridge University Press.

Bender, F. (2021). Enfranchising the disenfranchised: Should refugees receive political rights in liberal democracies? *Citizenship Studies*. 25(1), 56–71 . https://doi.org/10.1080/13621025.2020.1825625

Benhabib, S. (2004). *The Rights of Others: Aliens, Residents and Citizens*. Cambridge University Press.

Betts, A., & Collier, P. (2017). *Refuge: Rethinking Refugee Policy in a Changing World*. Oxford University Press.

Carens, J. (2013). *The Ethics of Immigration*. Oxford University Press.

Cherem, M. (2016). Refugee Rights: Against Expanding the Definition of a "Refugee" and Unilateral Protection Elsewhere. *Journal of Political Philosophy*, *24*(2), 183–205. https://doi.org/10.1111/jopp.12071

Ellis, A., & Et. Al. (2007). *Voting from Abroad: The International IDEA Handbook*. International Institute for Democracy and Electoral Assistance.

Erman, E. (2014), The Boundary Problem and the Ideal of Democracy. *Constellations*, 21: 535–546. https://doi.org/10.1111/1467-8675.12116

Fraser, N. (2008). Abnormal Justice. *Critical Inquiry*, *34*(3), 393–422. https://doi.org/10.1086/589478

Gibney, M. J. (2004). *The Ethics and Politics of Asylum: Liberal Democracy and Response to Refugees*. Cambridge University Press.

Goodin, R. (2007). Enfranchising All Affected Interests, and Its Alternatives. *Philosophy & Public Affairs*, *35*(1), 40–68. https://doi.org/10.1111/j.1088-4963.2007.00098.x

Hathaway, J. C. (2005). *The Rights of Refugees under International Law*. Cambridge University Press.

Kapelner, Z. (2020). Vulnerable minorities and democratic legitimacy in refugee admission. *Ethics & Global Politics*, *13*(1), 50–63. https://doi.org/10.1080/16544951.2020.1735016

Kymlicka, W. (2001). *Politics in the Vernacular: Nationalism, Multiculturalism and Citizenship*. Oxford University Press.

Lopez-Guerra, C. (2005). Should Expatriates Vote? *The Journal of Political Philosophy*, *13* (2), 218–227. https://doi.org/10.1111/j.1467-9760.2005.00221.x

Miller, D. (2009). Democracy's Domain. *Philosophy & Public Affairs*, *37*(3), 201–228. https://doi.org/10.1111/j.1088-4963.2009.01158.x

Miller, D. (2017). *Strangers in Our Midst: The Political Philosophy of Immigration*. Harvard University Press.

Miller, D. (2020). Reconceiving the democratic boundary problem. *Philosophy Compass*, *15*(11), 1–9. https://doi.org/10.1111/phc3.12707

Näsström, S. (2011). The Challenge of the All-Affected Principle. *Political Studies*, *59*(1), 116–134. https://doi.org/10.1111/j.1467-9248.2010.00845.x

Orgad, L. (2017). Naturalization. In A. Shachar, R. Bauböck, I. Bloemraad, & M. Vink (Eds.), *The Oxford Handbook of Citizenship* (pp. 337–358). Oxford University Press.

Owen, D. (2012). Constituting the polity, constituting the demos: On the place of the all affected interests principle in democratic theory and in resolving the democratic boundary problem. *Ethics & Global Politics, 5*(3), 129–152. https://doi.org/10.3402/egp.v5i3.18617

Owen, D. (2013). Citizenship and the marginalities of migrants. *Critical Review of International Social and Political Philosophy, 16*(3), 326–343. https://doi.org/10.1080/13698230.2013.795702

Owen, D. (2018). Populus, demos and self-rule. In D. Owen (Ed.), *Democratic Inclusion: Rainer Bauböck in Dialogue* (pp. 183–204). Manchester University Press.

Owen, D. (2019). Refugees, EU Citizenship and the Common European Asylum System: A Normative Dilemma for EU Integration. *Ethical Theory and Moral Practice, 22*(2), 347–369. https://doi.org/10.1007/s10677-019-09973-x

Owen, D. (2020). *What Do We Owe to Refugees?* Polity Press.

Pevnick, R. (2009). Social Trust and the Ethics of Immigration Policy. *The Journal of Political Philosophy, 17*(2), 146–167. https://doi.org/10.1111/j.1467-9760.2007.00296.x

Price, M. (2009). *Rethinking Asylum: History, Purpose and Limits*. Cambridge University Press.

Ragab, N. J., & Antara, L. (2018). *Political Participation of Refugees: The Case of Afghan and Syrian Refugees in Germany*. International Institute for Democracy and Electoral Assistance.

Sevinç, T. (2019). Three approaches to social unity and solidarity. *Critical Review of International Social and Political Philosophy*, . https://doi.org/10.1080/13698230.2019.1697843

Shachar, A. (2009). *The Birthright Lottery: Citizenship and Global Inequality*. Harvard University Press.

Shachar, A., & Hirschl, R. (2014). On Citizenship, States, and Markets. *The Journal of Political Philosophy, 22*(2), 231–257. https://doi.org/10.1111/jopp.12034

Shacknove, A. E. (1985). Who Is a Refugee? *Ethics, 95*(2), 274–284. https://doi.org/10.1086/292626

Song, S. (2009). Democracy and noncitizen voting rights. *Citizenship Studies, 13*(6), 607–620. https://doi.org/10.1080/13621020903309607

UN High Commissioner for Refugees (UNHCR). (2003). *Political Rights of Refugees*. (Report No, PPLA/2003/04) https://www.refworld.org/docid/3fe820794.html

UN High Commissioner for Refugees (UNHCR). (2011). *Convention and protocol relating to the status of refugees*. http://www.unhcr.org/3b66c2aa10.html

UN High Commissioner for Refugees (UNHCR). (2018). *'Refugees' and 'Migrants' Frequently Asked Questions (FAQs)* https://www.refworld.org/docid/56e81c0d4.html

Weil, P. (2001). Access to Citizenship: A Comparison of Twenty-Five Nationality Laws. In A. Aleinikoff & D. B. Klusmeyer (Eds.), *Citizenship Today: Global Perspectives and Practices* (pp. 17–35). Carnegie Endowment for International Peace.

Weinstock, D. (2001). Prospects for Transnational Citizenship and Democracy. *Ethics & International Affairs, 15*(2), 53–66. https://doi.org/10.1111/j.1747-7093.2001.tb00358.x

Ziegler, R. (2017). *Voting Rights of Refugees*. Cambridge University Press.

Legislative expatriate representation: A conditional defence of overseas constituencies

Marcus Carlsen Häggrot

ABSTRACT
Democracies that appoint legislators through elections in territorially defined, sub-national constituencies and simultaneously enfranchise expatriate citizens must either assign expatriate voters to in-country constituencies (assimilated representation) or group them into distinct overseas constituencies that elect their own legislators (discrete representation). This essay critically reviews extant normative discussions of the two models and develops a normative analysis of its own. This suggests that when expatriates form but a small part of a democracy's overall demos, discrete representation is the more attractive model of expatriate representation as it overall better satisfies four important standards of evaluation, namely: equal opportunities for political influence, deliberation within the legislature, deliberation among constituents, and partisan voter mobilisation. This argument is also defended against the potential objections that the said standards can be satisfied by other means than discrete expatriate representation and that the defence of discrete expatriate representation implies a proliferation of special constituencies.

Introduction

Numerous contemporary democracies employ geographically defined, local constituencies to elect members of the central, national legislature. That is to say, democracies typically parse their enfranchised citizenry, the demos, into a number of formally separate groups or *constituencies*,[1] which are in turn charged with electing a defined number of legislators. These constituencies can in principle be defined in an array of different ways – for example, in terms of citizens' age, profession, ethnicity, income, etc. – but contemporary democracies usually define their legislative constituencies in terms of location and place of residence such that affiliation with a given constituency normally tracks permanent residence in a particular area of the national territory. The first-past-the-post electoral system that is used in the United Kingdom (Mitchell, 2005) provides a paradigmatic example of this practice, but geographic constituencies feature in many other electoral systems too, for example, in the French two-round-run-off voting system (Elgie, 2005), in the German mixed-electoral system (Saalfeld, 2005), and in the multi-member-district proportional electoral system that is used in e.g. Spain (Hopkin, 2005). More generally, a survey study by Handley (2008) suggests that in 2005 geographic constituencies were used to elect some or all members of the legislature in no less than 84 countries.[2]

In addition to this, it is nowadays also common for democracies to enfranchise their non-resident, expatriate citizens[3] such that they can participate in the national legislative elections of their home country even though they permanently reside abroad. Once a rarity typically reserved for diplomatic, military and/or other official personnel posted abroad, expatriate enfranchisement has globally expanded since 1960s, and by the year 2016 expatriates were enfranchised for home-country legislative elections in 124 states (Caramani & Grotz, 2015; International Institute for Democracy and Electoral Assistance (IDEA), 2016).

The combination, though, of (legislative) expatriate enfranchisement and geographic constituencies gives rise to a practical conundrum. Expatriates do not reside anywhere within the national territory. As such, they are not eligible to enrol in any home state constituency, and their votes cannot therefore be counted towards the election of a legislator. At the same time, expatriates are meant to be members of the demos and to possess the opportunity to participate in legislative elections.

For resolving this conundrum, two basic solutions are available. The first, which Peter Spiro (2006) has aptly called 'assimilated representation', is to make a legislative or constitutional decision to let expatriate nationals register and poll 'through their last place of in-country residence' (p. 226) so that in effect, they participate in the election of representatives for in-country constituencies. The other option – labelled by Spiro as 'discrete representation' (p. 226) – is to gather all expatriate voters into distinct overseas constituencies that elect – for the home country legislature – a defined number of legislators who are returned by an exclusively expatriate electorate, but nevertheless have the same rights and voting strength in the legislature as the legislators returned by in-country constituencies.

However, assimilated and discrete expatriate representation both upset commonplace views and intuitions about what constituencies are and/or how they should be configured. Discrete representation is in tension with the in practice widely recognised norm that constituencies are congruent with, or simply are, geographic areas *within* the national territory. The assimilated representation, for its part, runs up against the intuition that constituencies are, or should be, be geographically contiguous (cf., Forest & Medeiros, 2020) for the affiliation of expatriates with geographic in-country constituencies entails that those constituencies get attached to them numerous individuals who are permanently at a remove from the relevant in-country area.

Yet, democratic societies cannot refrain from committing to one or the other model, and in an increasing number of democracies there is genuine political controversy about what model is to be favoured.

Until the mid-1970s, democracies with voting rights for expatriates seemingly adopted assimilated representation by default, and it still remains the more common model of expatriate representation (Collyer, 2014, p. 65). To give but a few examples from a long list, assimilated representation continues to be practiced in the United Kingdom, the USA, Canada, Brazil, Mexico, Germany, Spain, Switzerland, and Norway (cf., Collyer & Vathi, 2007). Assimilated expatriate representation is not the only game in town, though. Since its first introduction in Portugal in 1976 (Collyer, 2014), discrete representation has gained popularity and it is now implemented in Algeria, Cape Verde, Colombia, Croatia, the Dominican Republic, Ecuador, France, Italy, Macedonia, Mozambique, Niger, Portugal, Romania, Senegal, and Tunisia (Collyer, 2014, p. 68; Palop-García, 2018). A move to discrete expatriate representation is also under discussion in Peru, Spain, Uruguay, and Jamaica (Palop-García, 2018). So whether expatriate representation should be discrete or assimilated is a live political controversy for democratic societies, and hence it is of practical importance to think through the models' normative aspects: What are their merits and disadvantages? Is one model preferable to the other and if so, under what conditions?

The importance of subjecting discrete and assimilated expatriate representation to a normative analysis is further bolstered by recent developments in political and legal theory. In recent years, prominent theorists have come to the aid of expatriate voting and argued forcefully that the enfranchisement of expatriates is defensible on the grounds of democratic proceduralism (Rubio-Marin, 2006), stakeholder citizenship (Bauböck, 2007), the all-subjected principle (Owen, 2010), and/or on the grounds of context-specific considerations (Pogonyi, 2014). But again, there is no genuine opportunity to vote for expatriates if constituencies are defined territorially and there is no decision with respect to expatriates' constituency affiliation. So in order to hold a coherent position, advocates of expatriate enfranchisement have to ultimately commit either to discrete or assimilated expatriate representation, and exploring the models' normative aspects is hence a philosophically important task as well. Indeed, this is an integral part of what it is to take a philosophical stance in favour of expatriate enfranchisement.

For practical and philosophical reasons, then, it is important to subject discrete and assimilated expatriate representation to normative analysis. Yet, scholars have shown relatively little interest for the institutional structures that may render expatriate votes effective, and normative analyses of the constituency question remain sparse. The only systemic inquiries on the topic are by Spiro and Rainer Bauböck, who ultimately arrive at different conclusions. Spiro (2006) argues that discrete representation is 'the better mechanism' (p. 207), whereas Bauböck (2007) takes the opposite position that 'assimilated representation should be the default model' (p. 2433). However, there are significant shortcomings in both authors' arguments. The particular arguments that the scholars mobilise to support of their respective positions suffer from several flaws that I detail below, and the analyses are more generally incomplete in the sense that they lack what one might call an 'internal' analysis – an analysis that examines how discrete and assimilated expatriate representation relate to the values and objectives that are associated with the wider, territorial constituency scheme that both models are, after all, meant to complement.

In light of these shortcomings, then, the present essay proposes to look anew at the normative aspects of discrete and assimilated expatriate representation. In particular, it proposes to evaluate the models in terms of four democratic standards – equal opportunities of political influence, deliberation within the legislature, deliberation among constituents, and partisan voter mobilisation. The essay further argues that in an important set of cases, these standards are overall more thoroughly satisfied by discrete representation than assimilated representation, and the essay as such provides a systematic, normative defence of discrete expatriate representation.

To this defence attach a few caveats and limitations. First, some arguments in the essay presuppose a particular, social condition – i.e. that the democracy's expatriate electorate forms but a relatively small part of the overall demos. This condition does not hold across all contemporary democracies. But as is explained below, it is characteristic of a sizable set of democratic states. It is for this set only that the essay defends discrete expatriate representation, and as such the defence is *conditional*.

Further, the essay advocates discrete expatriate representation on the grounds of several democratic values, but these are not defended *per se*. As an investigation into the institutions that are appropriate for realising expatriate enfranchisement, the essay further presumes that expatriate voting is permissible, possibly even desirable. But this controversial background view (cf., Beckman 2009; Lopez-Guerra, 2005) is not defended either. The essay thus offers a distinctively *intramural* argument that aims to persuade those readers only who grant that equal opportunities for political influence, deliberation, and partisan voter mobilisation are valid ethical objectives and, further, that expatriate enfranchisement is legitimate.

Third, the essay develops a *pro-tanto* defence of discrete expatriate representation. As such, it leaves open the possibility that once all relevant aspects considered, discrete representation is not, after all, the most attractive policy choice. But the argument is nonetheless important, for democratic considerations presumably weigh heavily when it comes to the design of democratic institutions.

Fourth, the present argument is largely a theoretic one. To show that discrete expatriate representation realises certain values better than assimilated representation, one must in principle show that the models demonstrably perform in certain ways with respect to the relevant standards. But apart from a few single-case studies (Collard & Webb, 2020; Gauja, 2020; Kalu & Scarrow, 2020) and one small-N study (Østergaard-Nielsen & Ciornei, 2019), it is still under-researched and ill-understood what empirical effects the different forms of expatriate representation actually produce (Østergaard-Nielsen & Ciornei, 2019, p. 153). The argument must therefore primarily rely on *a-priori* considerations as to how the models might, or might not, satisfy the relevant standards, and it thus constitutes an expressly theoretic argument for discrete expatriate representation.

Finally, it is important to note that the argument does not offer a complete blueprint for implementing discrete expatriate representation. It takes no view on the number of constituencies that expatriates should form, on how large the constituency (or constituencies) should be in terms of population, or on how many legislator expatriates should be allowed to elect. These are practically and normatively important questions, not least because constituency size and magnitude jointly determine how the influence of a vote cast in one constituency compares to that of votes cast elsewhere. But these are questions of implementation that arise only after it is decided that expatriates shall form a special constituency. The essay therefore brackets these questions and focuses exclusively on the more fundamental and still controversial issue whether expatriates shall have discrete representation at all.

The remainder of the essay is structured as follows. Section 2 reviews Spiro's and Bauböck's respective defences of assimilated and discrete expatriate representation. It highlights the arguments' specific shortcomings, and develops the more general critique that in extant thinking about expatriates' constituency affiliation, there has been insufficient attention to how the different constituency models relate to the values and objectives that are associated with, or internal to, the more general, territorial constituency framework that both discrete and assimilated representation are meant to complement. Section 3 goes on to argue that in evaluating the different forms of expatriate representation, one should pay particular attention to how thoroughly the models satisfy four distinct standards – i.e. equal opportunity of political influence, deliberation within the legislature, deliberation among constituents, and partisan voter mobilisation. These standards are argued to be particularly suitable as they are at once reflective of generally democratic values and reflective of values that are arguably associated with the territorial definition of parliamentary constituencies. Section 4 then uses the four standards to assess assimilated and discrete expatriate representation and shows that when expatriates form but a small part of the demos, discrete representation is the overall more reliable means to satisfy the standards. This suggests the conclusion that under certain conditions the discrete representation is the more defensible model of the expatriate representation, but this can be challenged from two different directions. It might be claimed that the standards used in this analysis can be satisfied by other means than discrete expatriate representation, and it might be objected that the defence leads to an unchecked proliferation of special constituencies. Section 5 critically discusses these challenges, and section 6 concludes with a summary of the argument.

Extant Discussions of Assimilated and Discrete Expatriate Representation

Normative analyses of discrete and assimilated expatriate representation are sparse, but focused, express analyses have been developed by Spiro, who ultimately advocates discrete expatriate representation, and Bauböck, who defends assimilated representation. What is the content of these arguments and how do they stand up to scrutiny?

With respect to discrete expatriate representation, Spiro's main argument is that unless the expatriate citizenry is very small or politically unengaged, it is 'the better mechanism' since it enables the transmission of expatriates' distinct interests into the legislature and brings it about that their 'distinct interests [are] represented in national decision-making' (Spiro, 2006, p. 227).

Spiro additionally notes that insofar as expatriates are represented discretely, overseas constituencies can be made larger, population-wise, than in-country constituencies. In turn, this form of malapportionment limits the electoral influence that expatriates can exercise over home-country politics. It helps ensure that expatriate voters do not 'overwhelm resident electorates' (Spiro, 2006, p. 228) and that home country politics continues to be dominated by domestically resident voters. Spiro regards this as proper because in his view domestically resident citizens have greater stakes in home country politics (Spiro, 2006, p. 228). Thus, he seems to endorse discrete expatriate representation for the additional reason also that it has an ability to moderate, or keep in reasonable proportion, the electoral influence of expatriates over home country politics – and in this he shares ground with Michael Tager, who in a passing comment suggests that discrete expatriate representation might be desirable since it 'would generally prevent expatriates from having too decisive a role in the politics of states they no longer live in' (Tager, 2006, p. 57).

Assimilated expatriate representation, for its part, is the model favoured by Bauböck, and the argument here is heavily informed by Bauböck's distinctive stakeholder-justification of expatriate enfranchisement. Expatriates, on this account, have a claim to enfranchisement because they share with in-country citizens the empirical condition of being stakeholders in the polity such that their future well-being importantly depends on the flourishing of that polity (Bauböck, 2007, p. 2422). And Bauböck's further thought now seems to be that assimilated expatriate representation is desirable because it is particularly true to this fundamental rationale for expatriate enfranchisement and, indeed, helps to publicise the stakeholdership of expatriates. Assimilated representation, Bauböck seems to reason, entails that expatriates participate electorally through the same mechanisms as domestically resident citizens. Assimilated representation thus brings it about that expatriates are '*seen as* voting for legislators who will represent the general citizenry'; it helps to affirm publicly that expatriates 'share with domestic citizens the same interest in the future of the polity', and on Bauböck's view, this is the very reason why 'assimilated representation should be the default model' (p. 2433).

The three arguments just outlined are the most explicit and focused defences in the literature of discrete and assimilated expatriate representation, respectively. But none of them is satisfactory. This is most obvious, perhaps, with Spiro's argument from interest representation. It presupposes that expatriate interest representation in the legislature is a valid normative objective. A rationale for this proposition is not provided, though, and so one has no more reason to accept that proposition than one has reason to accept the counter-stipulation that expatriate interests should be kept out of the legislature. Of course, Spiro might reply to this by furnishing the presently missing argument. As a matter of fact, one might read parts of what follows as an attempt to do just that. But such a revisionary project can only get off the ground if we first recognise that Spiro's original statement of the argument is incomplete and, therefore, unpersuasive.

Spiro's interest-argument is not the only one with serious shortcomings, though. This is true as well for Bauböck's argument from stakeholdership. For one thing, this argument presupposes that it is a good thing if electoral institutions, and the constituency plan in particular, help to publicise that expatriate citizens share with in-country citizens the condition of stakeholdership. But why is this? A potential reply might be that such publicization helps to entrench and consolidate in people's minds the enfranchisement of expatriates. To a degree, this seems a fair enough view, but it does presuppose that electoral institutions, and constituencies in particular, should play a role in stabilising or entrenching the franchise, either in general or for particular groups. This is a questionable view. Of course, it is no bad thing if a constituency plan helps to build popular support for the enfranchisement of a particular group, but there is a risk here that the constituency plan gets unduly burdened with normative expectations that are maybe better taken care of by other means than constituency design.

Additionally, it is not obvious, as Bauböck seems to think, that as compared to discrete expatriate representation, assimilated representation is better able to publicise expatriates' stakeholdership. If a democracy divides its in-country electorate into a number of territorial, subnational constituencies, it is arguable that the discrete representation of expatriates is a logical extension of this practice as voters here continue to be grouped on the basis of residence. And seen from this perspective, it might well be that also under discrete representation, expatriates are generally seen as voters who play by the ordinary electoral rules and share with domestic citizens the condition of stakeholdership.

This finally leaves us with the argument by Spiro (and Tager) that discrete expatriate representation is desirable since it helps to contain expatriates' electoral influence on home country politics. Unlike the two previous arguments, this one is a fair enough argument on its own terms – or so much I grant for now. Yet, there is an ostensible tension between this argument and the general democratic commitment to equal opportunity of political influence – i.e. the idea that citizens should all have the same electoral and non-electoral opportunities to exercise influence on political decisions. Perhaps this tension can be resolved by an argument that emphasises expatriates' limited liability to coercive home state power. Even so, democrats might be uneasy about a defence of an institutional arrangement that expressly points to how the arrangement curbs the influence of particular citizens and limits their influence to a level lower than that available to other citizens. Presumably, many democrats might want to use this only as an argument of last resort, or as an argument that works alongside others. More generally, the point is that it is potentially controversial how much weight one should ascribe to the moderated-influence argument, and that it therefore does not constitute a fully satisfactory argument for discrete expatriate representation either.

The critical points developed so far should suffice to establish that extant normative discussions of discrete and assimilated expatriate representation are unsatisfactory and need revisiting. Still, I want to underscore a last point that is more general. Roughly, this is that extant thinking about the normative attributes of discrete and assimilate expatriate representation is incomplete. Nowhere in the scholarship is there an appreciation that both discrete and assimilated expatriate representation fundamentally serve to integrate expatriate voters into a pre-existing, wider system of territorially defined, electoral constituencies, and there is no attempt, either, to see how the different forms of expatriate representation might help to sustain, or might hazard, the values or objectives that this wider system serves. Yet, this kind of analysis is part of the task. Absent any special countervailing considerations, we should want our model of expatriate representation to cohere at the normative, principled level with the wider institutional framework of which it is a part. Accordingly, it is not sufficient to examine how the two models relate to general evaluative standards as, e.g. stakeholdership; we must also look at how they relate to the values and objectives that are internal to the wider, territorial-constituency scheme. But Spiro, Bauböck, and others who write about expatriate representation roundly fail to conduct this type of internal analysis. Their analyses and respective defences are thus incomplete, independently of their more particular shortcomings, and the task of this essay is accordingly to rethink more carefully and systematically the ethics of expatriate representation.

Four evaluative standards

In order to think through the normative aspects of the assimilated-vs-discrete representation choice, I propose to use four evaluative standards and ultimately favour the model of expatriate representation that most robustly secures, or realises, equal opportunities (for citizens) for political influence, deliberation within the legislature, deliberation among constituents, and partisan voter mobilisation.

One reason these four benchmarks are particularly apt for the task at hand is that they reflect deeply *democratic* values and objectives. Equal opportunity for political influence is widely regarded as a core democratic value and is expressly endorsed by prominent theorists of democracy such as Rawls (1973, pp. 224, 221), Thompson (2002, p. 9), Christiano (2008, p. 95), and Kolodny (2014, p. 227).

Much the same is true for deliberation, which we can define broadly as 'mutual communication that involves weighing and reflecting on preferences, values, and interests relevant to common concerns' (Mansbridge, 2015, p. 27). The importance of deliberation, notably in the legislature, was already stressed by Burke (1996, p. 69-70), Bentham (1999, p. 16 n), and Mill ([1861] 2008, pp. 104–5). And more recently, deliberative democrats have argued that deliberation is a generally valuable, democratic practice that helps to generate legitimacy (Cohen, 1989), that publicises citizens' mutual respect for each other (Gutmann & Thompson, 2004), and which helps to identify substantially good policy decisions (Landemore, 2012).

Finally, one can hardly overestimated how important practices of partisan voter mobilisation are to an electoral democracy. Hustings, town-hall meetings, door-to-door campaigning, media appearances, political billposting, and other forms of partisan voter mobilisation all provide voters with information about candidates and/or the parties that stand in an election. Campaigns also help to motivate voters to turn out on election day, they are a form of interaction that gives citizens a certain power over the future decisions of their legislators, and so they form an integral part of electoral democracy that should, indeed, be recognised as valuable, democratic practices (cf., Beerbohm, 2016).

The four benchmarks against which I propose to evaluate discrete and assimilated expatriate representation are thoroughly democratic; then, and as such they seem particularly apt for guiding our thinking about the institutional design of electoral institutions. But this is not all.

The four standards I propose to utilise are not only associated with democratic rule in general, but also more specifically with the territorial definition of parliamentary constituencies. Let me unpack this some more, starting with the value of partisan voter mobilisation.

A territorial definition of constituencies entails that the members of every parliamentary constituency are gathered and, indeed, concentrated within a contiguous and clearly delimited space. This concentration, in turn, makes it relatively easy or inexpensive for electoral candidates to hold townhall meetings, to engage in door-to-door campaigning, to distribute political advertisement in broadcast media, and so forth. And given this facilitation, there is arguably an important sense in which territorial constituencies 'enable political campaigning' (Rehfeld, 2005, p. 174) and protect partisan voter mobilisation practices (cf., Williams, 1998, p. 234).

The geographic concentration of constituents is also important for the occurrence of deliberation among constituents. By gathering those who belong to the same constituency in one particular area, territorial constituencies make it relatively easy for members of the same constituency to meet and talk with each other, and thus also to deliberate. Given that nowadays electoral districts typically have many thousands of members, territorial constituencies cannot, for sure, be expected to sustain deliberation comprehensively, between *all* members of the relevant constituency. But the concentration of constituents can plausibly be expected to result in deliberation among a subset of citizens within each constituency. As Rehfeld (2005) puts it, 'in each *neighbourhood*, we might see real deliberation about candidates and policies. . . . indeed today many citizens attend candidate meetings that are held nearby and discuss politics with their neighbors' (p. 172; emphasis added), and so we may plausibly regard territorial constituencies as enablers of deliberation between constituents (cf., Schwartz, 1988, p. 13).

Further, when constituencies are defined on the basis of geography, legislators are elected by distinctively local electorates that reside in a particular area. Geographically differentiated electorates, in turn, are likely to have at least somewhat disparate interests, political judgements, and lived experiences. Different locales often have different physical landscapes or different climates. They are likely to harbour different types of economic activity and relatedly, their inhabitants are likely to have dissimilar socioeconomic profiles. Different areas within a country may additionally be homelands for culturally, linguistically, or religiously distinct groups. The result of geographic constituencies is thus most likely that legislators, in response to actual or perceive electoral rewards, articulate in the legislature a broad variety of concerns and judgements (cf., Rehfeld, 2005, pp. 151–53) and so turn the legislature into a diverse body that harbours a range of different interests, facts, and political judgements.

Such informational and perspectival diversity, in turn, is closely linked with the practice of deliberation. Because deliberation is collective *reflection* – that is to say, *careful, earnest* thinking about the preferences, values, and interests bearing on collective issues (cf., Mansbridge, 2015, p. 29), it is presumably enhanced, or rendered more likely, to the extent that would-be deliberators are led to suspend, at least temporarily, their preconceptions about what interests and judgements are at stake in a given problem, what interests and judgements are legitimate, etc. and they are helped to see the issue from a different vantage point. Diversity in the deliberators' initial viewpoints arguably fosters this process of careful self-detachment and re-consideration, and perspectival diversity thus appears as a felicitous condition of deliberation. Naturally, such diversity may be not *sufficient* for there to be deliberation, but initial diversity in interests, judgements, and knowledge probably is a facilitating or enabling condition for careful consideration (cf., Mansbridge, 2015, p. 42; Sunstein, 1991; Young, 1993; Phillips, 1998, p. 159), and so it is arguable that territorial constituencies, which help to create just this sort diversity in the legislature, help to sustain the value of legislative deliberation.

This finally brings us to the value of equal opportunities for political influence. Territorial constituencies promote this principle because they help to bring about a particular distribution of legislator attention. As local constituencies engender that legislators must seek election from the voters of a particular area within the country, they encourage legislators to *not* all direct their gaze and attention at the very same population groups within demos – e.g. the populations that are generally well-off, well-educated, and electorally active. Instead, legislators are given incentives to spread their attention to separate parts of the national territory, and territorial constituencies thus help to bring about a relatively even distribution of legislator attention such that citizens are objects of legislator attention in a roughly equal measure.

The equal spread of legislator attention is, in turn, an enabler of equal opportunity of political influence. This is so because some – though not all – of the important ways in which citizens may exercise political influence presuppose that the relevant citizens enjoy or receive some legislator attention. For example, I can only influence politics by writing letters to members of the legislature if legislators notice the letter, open and read it, and mentally register the message. The addressed legislators need not agree with the message or adopt the position the letter advocates. But for there to be a genuine opportunity to exercise political influence by the means of letter-writing, it is indispensable that the letter author is granted some basic attention by legislators. Similar points apply to other important forms of exercising political influence, for example, conversations with legislators or demonstrations aiming at members of the legislature. Legislator attention is thus a precondition for some of the important ways citizens exercise political influence, and equal opportunity for political influence is thus enhanced to the extent that legislator attention distributes evenly across the demos. Territorial constituencies arguably help to secure such an even distribution of legislator attention, and as a result it is arguable that territorial constituencies promote equal opportunity for political influence.

Equal opportunity for political influence, legislative deliberation, constituent deliberation, and partisan voter mobilisation are evaluative standards, then, that at once reflect general democratic values and values that are associated with the territorial constituency scheme. And as such, these standards seem particularly apt for the task at hand: They enable us to both pick out the form of expatriate representation that is most attractive on democratic grounds and to identify the model of expatriate representation that coheres best with the normative logic of the wider constituency plan that both assimilated and discrete expatriate representation serve to complement.

The conditional case for discrete expatriate representation

As we move along now to assess assimilated and discrete expatriate representation respectively, it will be helpful to look first at assimilated representation.

Two basic points are worth noting right away. First, we assume for the purpose of this essay that the number of expatriate electors is relatively small as compared to the home state's domestic electorate. To be sure, this condition does not hold across all democracies. In the case of Malta, for example, a relatively recent estimate suggests that slightly more than 20% of the citizenry lives abroad (Hutcheson & Arrighi, 2015, p. 891), and a significant number of other democracies likely feature similar, or even higher, rates of expatriation. This notwithstanding, there exists a set of democratic states in which expatriates form a relatively small part of the overall demos. According to the estimates of Hutcheson and Arrighi (2015), expatriates make up no more than 5% of the total citizenry in Spain, France, Sweden, the Czech Republic, Denmark, Germany, Belgium, and Italy. Their estimates further suggest that in Hungary, Finland, the Netherlands, Slovakia, Austria, Slovenia, the United Kingdom, Greece, and Poland, expatriates form no more than 9% of these states' total citizenry (p. 891). So within the set of states that qualify as democracies, there is a subset – which is not necessarily exhausted by the European states studied by Hutcheson and Arrighi – that is characterised by comparatively low rates of expatriation, and this is the set of cases the essay focuses upon.

Second, the characteristic feature of assimilated expatriate representation is that it assigns expatriate voters to in-country constituencies such that they effectively poll through their last in-country place of residence. In conjunction with the first point, this means that assimilated expatriate representation has particular consequences for the make-up of parliamentary constituencies. So long as the expatriate electorate is a relatively small part of the overall demos, assimilated expatriate representation entails that most, or all, in-country constituencies comprise small enclaves of expatriate voters, who are potentially scattered across the entire globe.[4]

This point about how assimilated expatriate representation creates small expat enclaves within in-country constituencies is important for how the model performs in terms of the four benchmarks we are interested in. Indeed, it is a central reason why this model can only realise imperfectly the values of legislative deliberation, constituent deliberation, partisan voter mobilisation and equal opportunity for political influence. Let me develop these points in the stated order.

When expatriates form small enclaves within in-country constituencies – constituencies that are numerically dominated by domestically resident citizens – legislators face relatively weak incentives to bring into the legislature any interests, political judgments, or experiences that are specific to expatriate citizens. Expatriates being few in every constituency, they cannot pretend to form a reservoir of potential votes in upcoming elections and legislators will have little to win on bringing their distinct viewpoints and concerns into the legislature. Legislators will moreover have relatively few occasions to meet expatriates and to learn about their specific interests and viewpoints. If expatriates form but small enclaves within in-country constituencies, each legislator is likely to mostly interact with domestically resident electors. Interaction with expatriates is likely to remain somewhat exceptional – in part, maybe, because of the logistics of such interaction, but more importantly because of the sheer numbers and the expatriates' small-minority status. Legislators thus have quite poor opportunities to learn about, for example, the distinctive interests that expatriates might have in well-functioning consular services, the particular political judgements that expatriates might have about the home country's foreign policy, or, maybe, about how immigration regulations in the home country affect expatriates' ability to return together with their partner, spouse, and family.

So, insofar as expatriates form small enclaves with in-country constituencies, legislators are likely to be both uninterested in, and uninformed about, expatriates' interests, political judgements, and living conditions, and assimilated expatriate representation is thus likely to make the legislature a perspectivally and informationally poorer environment than it could be. True, legislators will tend to articulate in the legislature the interests and judgments that are specific to their local, domestically resident electorates and so create a geographic diversity of voices that supports deliberation. Yet, expatriate perspectives are likely to be marginal, if present at all, and the value of deliberation will therefore be dented: Legislative deliberation is realised to a degree, but not to its full potential.

A similar point applies to deliberation among constituents. Because territorial in-country constituencies enable what Rehfeld has styled neighbourhood deliberation, there is a sense in which assimilated expatriate representation sustains deliberation among constituents. But with expatriates, the situation is rather different. Expatriates cannot, for obvious reasons, participate in the neighbourhood deliberations that occur domestically, within the respective in-country constituencies. Because expatriates often live at significant distance from each other, they also face obstacles to deliberating amongst themselves. And even if distance is no problem, expatriates will often belong to different constituencies as they have emigrated from different parts of the home country. British expatriates in Berlin, for example, mostly likely belong to different constituencies in the UK. As such, they cannot engage in constituent deliberation proper, and assimilated expatriate representation thus entails that the benchmark is satisfied only imperfectly. Assimilated expatriate representation promotes deliberation amongst constituents, but not fully so.

The existence of small, globally dispersed expat enclaves poses difficulties for partisan voter mobilisation as well. The potentially global dispersal of the enclave members means that classic voter mobilisation techniques such as billposting, meet-and-greet actions, townhall meetings, etc. are impracticable with respect to expatriate voters. The thin scattering of expatriate voters into diverse in-country constituencies also means that for candidates and parties there are virtually no electoral rewards to trying to mobilise expatriates. So even if expatriate voter mobilisation can in part proceed by digital or other means – e.g. phone calls or emails to expatriate citizens, live-streamed townhall meetings – it is unlikely that under assimilated expatriate representation voter mobilisation is directed to any significant degree towards expatriates.

This expectation also receives some support from empirical observations. In three recent single-case studies on the overseas activities of Australian, British, and US political parties, respectively, it has been observed that in each of these democracies expatriate representation is assimilated, and that in each case, the political parties' investment in party abroad work is 'relatively modest' (Gauja, 2020, p. 874), 'weak' (Collard & Webb, 2020, p. 16) or 'low' (Kalu & Scarrow, 2020, p. 897). Single-case studies as these do not, of course, permit conclusions about general co-variance, let alone causality, but they do lend plausibility to view that assimilated expatriate representation is probably unfavourable to partisan mobilisation aimed at expatriates, and they bolster the *a priori* expectation that where expatriate representation is assimilated, the objective of partisan voter mobilisation is serviced only imperfectly.

Finally, we have in the previous section seen that citizens need to be objects of basic legislator attention in order to have opportunities for non-electoral political influence. But if expatriate voters form small enclaves within in-country constituencies, legislators are unlikely to have any attention to spare for them. Because of their small size, the expatriate enclaves are electorally unprofitable and legislators will tend to predominantly direct their attention at their local, in-country constituents. The result is that expatriates are likely to have worse opportunities for political influence than domestically resident citizens, and assimilated expatriate representation thus appears as a not-fully-egalitarian model of representation that fails to completely equalise citizens' opportunities for political influence.

Assimilated expatriate representation appears, then, as a democratically imperfect model of representation that does not fully realise the four democratic values that are arguably associated with the general, territorial system of representation. But does discrete representation fare any better?

With respect to constituent deliberation this is difficult to gauge. Discrete expatriate representation entails that expatriates are collected into a single, world-wide overseas constituency or, alternatively, into several overseas constituencies that cover different regions of the world. In any event, the arrangement guarantees that expatriates who live close to each other (e.g. in London) belong to the same overseas constituency, and hence it is arguable that discrete expatriate representation enables deliberation not only in neighbourhoods within the home country, but also in expatriate clubs and churches, in cultural associations, among expatriate friends, and in any other associations that might exist between the expatriates of the relevant country. As seen already, this contrasts with assimilated representation, where expatriates are likely to belong to different in-country constituencies although they live in the very same areas, and so there is some reason to think that discrete expatriate representation enables constituent deliberation more reliably than assimilated representation.

Yet, it is important to not overstate this point. Even in a system such as the French, which boasts 11 different constituencies for French expatriates, out-of-country constituents remain scattered across large areas that span several different countries, sometimes even continents, and so the potential for deliberation within these constituencies remains limited. Internet-based deliberation might, of course, help expatriates to bridge some of the distance that separates them from each other (see e.g. Bernal, 2010). But fora, social media, and other online-tools probably do not create as large contact surfaces and opportunities for deliberation between people as does spatial proximity and therefore, overseas constituencies should not be expected to deliver constituent deliberation on the same scale as ordinary, in-country constituencies, not even in the age of internet.

Additionally, there is a consideration to suggest that discrete representation might actually undermine forms of deliberation that the assimilated model leaves intact. So long as expatriates vote through their last place of in-country residence, expatriates can deliberate with co-constituents whenever they are in touch with persons who remain in that location, e.g. family members, friends, former colleagues, etc. But under discrete representation, expatriates and domestically resident citizens are sorted into distinct constituencies, and any pre-existing contacts between expatriates and home country residents thus become unable to function as conduits for constituent deliberation. In such contacts, there might, of course, be talk of politics, but since the interacting persons do not belong to the same constituency, it does not represent constituent deliberation *proper*.

The record of discrete expatriate representation is thus mixed with respect to the value of constituent deliberation. In one regard it is arguable that discrete representation secures or enhances constituent deliberation; from another perspective it appears that discrete representation undercuts forms of constituent deliberation. How much weight these competing considerations should be given in relation to each other is hard to determine, and so it remains largely unclear whether discrete expatriate representation really is any better at promoting constituent deliberation than assimilated representation.

With respect to equal opportunity of political influence, partisan voter mobilisation, and legislative deliberation, the picture is more determinate, though.

The discrete model of expatriate representation creates constituencies that are all-expatriate, and some legislators must thus seek election from an electorate that is entirely composed of expatriates. This gives the relevant legislators a strong incentive to primarily direct their attention at the expatriate community, and out-of-country citizens are thus virtually guaranteed to benefit from focused legislator attention. Meanwhile, in-country citizens continue to attract focused attention from the legislators that are elected in the various in-country constituencies. Discrete expatriate representation thus results in a distribution of legislator attention that is more even between in-country and out-of-country citizens than it is under assimilated representation, and so discrete representation arguably protects equal opportunities for political influence more robustly than does assimilated representation.

Much the same applies to partisan voter mobilisation. The existence of all-expatriate constituencies gives some legislative candidates an extremely strong incentive to aim their campaign activities at the expatriate electorate. Those who run for office in overseas constituencies are effectively obliged to hold their mobilisation activities abroad. Because of the constituents' wide dispersal, this is certainly a logistical challenge, and it cannot be expected that partisan voter mobilisation occurs as intensively in overseas constituencies as in in-country constituencies. But given the way it structures some candidates' incentives, discrete expatriate representation is still likely to be more conducive to political campaigning abroad than assimilated representation, and the objective of partisan voter mobilisation thus seems to be protected more thoroughly – both domestically and abroad – by discrete expatriate representation.

The point above about how discrete representation structures candidates' and legislators' incentives is also relevant when it comes to deliberation between legislators. Because of its particular incentive effects, discrete expatriate representation likely entails that some members of the legislature – i.e. those from overseas constituencies – will want to articulate in the legislature the interests, judgments, and experiences that are specific to their expatriate constituents. Distinct overseas constituencies also entail that the legislators of these constituencies will interact on regular basis with expatriates and so can develop a thorough knowledge of expatriates' living conditions, their distinctive interests, and political judgments. The discrete representation of expatriates thus makes it likely that expatriate perspectives are routinely articulated in the legislature, alongside the local, in-country perspectives that are put forward by legislators of in-country constituencies. This expectation also receives some empirical support from Østergaard-Nielsen and Ciornei (2019), who in a recent small-N study find that as compared to assimilated representation, discrete expatriate representation 'increases the incidence ratio of emigration-related parliamentary questions' (p. 161) and is also 'a strong predictor of emigration salience in [legislative] proposals' (p. 164). Discrete expatriate representation thus seems to render more diverse than assimilated representation the perspectives that come to the fore in the legislature, and in that way it seems to sustain legislative deliberation more reliably and thoroughly than does assimilated representation.

Overall, then, discrete expatriate representation seems to compare favourably to assimilated expatriate representation. It is not fully clear how the models compare in terms of realising constituent deliberation. But there are strong considerations to suggest that discrete expatriate representation delivers more reliably than assimilated representation on equal opportunity for political influence, partisan voter mobilisation, and legislative deliberation. And thus, there is a conditional, but nevertheless important, case in favour the discrete representation model: So long as expatriates form a relatively small part of the democracy's total demos, discrete expatriate representation is preferable both on democratic grounds and on the grounds of the values that are associated with the more general, territorial constituency scheme.

Objections and replies

The present defence of discrete expatriate representation is inevitably controversial, and two objections to it are especially important. The first one hones in on discrete expatriate representation and suggests that, in fact, it is not *necessary* to thoroughly realise democratic values. Legislative deliberation, for example, might be sustained robustly, not only through discrete expatriate representation, but also through an arrangement whereby expatriate viewpoints are carried into the legislature by, e.g. the foreign office or, alternatively, consultative expatriate bodies that must be heard by parliament whenever relevant legislation is proposed (cf., Bauböck, 2007, pp. 2433–4). Corresponding arrangements might also be found for the other standards discussed and a critic might therefore think that the present defence does not successfully vindicate discrete expatriate representation.

However, there are two things to be said in response. First, the essay does not claim to show that discrete expatriate representation is superior to *every* other institutional arrangement. It only looks at discrete and assimilated representation *per se*, and it argues that in this particular comparison, discrete representation comes out on top. If assimilated representation is modified and complemented with provisions for consultative bodies and other add-on arrangements and that revised arrangement turns out to satisfy our evaluative standards, then that is an interesting finding. But it does not invalidate the claim of the essay.

More importantly still, it is not clear what add-ons to assimilated representation might help with respect to partisan voter mobilisation and equal opportunity for political influence. That some expatriate interests and political judgments can be picked up and relayed by the foreign office administration or consultative expatriate bodies seems fair enough. But it is harder to see what particular add-ons might help with ensuring that legislator attention is spread evenly across in-country and out-of-country citizens. The point applies even more powerfully to partisan voter mobilisation: What arrangements other than discrete representation presentation can possibly help to bring partisan voter mobilisation into expatriate communities located abroad? So long as the critic does not furnish institutionally determinate answers to these questions, their challenge remains speculative and, as such, uncompelling.

The other challenge that might be brought against the present defence of discrete expatriate representation is that at least in theory, it implies an unchecked proliferation of special constituencies. If expatriates, so the challenge goes, are allowed to claim a constituency of their own, then there is nothing to stop other groups from doing the same. The present argument indeed implies that such claims for special constituencies must be accepted and that just about any sub-group in society should be afforded discrete representation if it so wishes. But this surely is implausible.

This objection ignores, however, that the present defence of discrete expatriate representation rests on a particular rationale. The essay advocates overseas constituencies for the specific reasons that (a) assimilated representation for expatriates likely hazards a set of important goals and that (b) discrete representation can likely remedy those hazards and help to robustly realise legislative deliberation, equal opportunity for political influence, and partisan voter mobilisation. The present argument as such implies that special constituencies are warranted if, and only if, groups can show, *mutatis mutandis*, that both reasons (a) and (b) apply to them, too.

Now, whether reasons (a) and (b) apply in any particular case has to be established through an analysis that attends to its specifics, and so it cannot be anticipated with precision for which groups the present argument legitimises special constituencies and for which it does not. Yet, it is safe to think that not all sub-groups in society will be able to demonstrate that both (a) and (b) apply to it. As an example, consider the case of women. In some jurisdictions, it is arguable that women's interests and political judgements are insufficiently represented in the legislature. It might also be thought that dedicated, 'women-only' constituencies can remedy this and can help improve deliberations within the legislature. But such dedicated constituencies may not bring it about that women experience more, or better, partisan mobilisation. Parties' and candidates' campaigning patterns might be just the same regardless of whether women form special constituencies or belong to mixed-gender, geographic constituencies. Women as a group cannot, then, demonstrate that both reasons (a) and (b) apply to them. This probably holds true for other groups as well, although the reasons for this might be different. For instance, it is conceivable that if the members of some group are collected into a dedicated constituency, there are benefits in terms of partisan mobilisation but not necessarily in terms of legislative diversity and deliberation. Be that as it may, the general point is that the present defence of expatriate constituencies only lends support to dedicated constituencies for non-expatriate groups if those groups have structurally similar features as expatriates and if special constituencies for those groups bring the same set of benefits as dedicated expatriate constituencies. Case-by-case analysis may reveal that this is demonstrable for some groups. But it certainly is not demonstrable for all, and thus it is an exaggeration to claim that the essay argument justifies an unchecked multiplication of special constituencies.

Conclusion

Should the legislative representation of expatriate voters be discrete or assimilated? This essay has argued that the question should be determined in part by looking at how well the respective models realise equal opportunity of political influence, constituent and legislative deliberation, and the objective of partisan voter mobilisation. It has further shown that if the expatriate electorate forms a relatively small share of the overall demos, discrete representation is probably the more reliable way to sustain equal opportunity of political influence, partisan voter mobilisation, and deliberation within the legislature. As such, the essay has made a conditional, *pro tanto* case for discrete expatriate representation, which it also has defended against two potential objections. By developing this case, the essay has addressed a question that in practice preoccupies democratic societies around the globe, but has not received adequate theorisation yet.

Notes

1. Constituency here means 'the group of people that is eligible to vote for a representative, representatives, or a political party' (Rehfeld, 2005, p. 36). For a disambiguation and discussion of other conceptions of constituency, see, Rehfeld (2005, Chapter 2) and James (2015).
2. Handley's study explicitly claims that of 87 surveyed countries 60 elect legislators through local constituencies the boundaries of which are periodically redrawn (Handley, 2008, p. 266). The underlying descriptive data (Handley, 2008, appendix B) reveals, though, that another 24 countries in the sample employ local constituencies that have permanently fixed boundaries. Legislators are thus drawn from local constituencies in a total of 84 countries.
3. In what follows, the terms non-resident citizens and expatriates are used interchangeably to refer generally to people who live abroad, outside of their state of nationality. In contrast to how the term is used sometimes in common parlance, 'expatriates' is meant to pick out neither nationals of particular countries nor workers who are especially highly skilled.
4. There is one situation where assimilated expatriate representation may not, in fact, result in the creation of small expat enclaves within in-country constituencies, even if the expatriate numbers are relatively low. This is if emigration from a country is specific to a region within it, and that patter of emigration remains stable over time. The emigrant population will then largely come from the same area within the home country, assimilated expatriate representation then entails that the emigrant electorate is largely assigned to a few select in-country constituencies, in which the emigrants may form sizable groups. But

presumably, this is an exceptional condition that we can bracket for the present analysis.

Acknowledgments

For comments on an earlier version of this essay, I am grateful to Ayelet Shachar, Ran Hirschl, Benjamin Boudou, Regina Schidel, Dominic Roser, Ali Emre Benli, Julian Culp, and the participants of the MANCEPT workshop 'Constituencies Revisited'. I also thank the two anonymous reviewers for their very helpful comments.

Disclosure statement

No potential conflict of interest was reported by the author(s).

ORCID

Marcus Carlsen Häggrot http://orcid.org/0000-0003-2476-0453

References

Bauböck, R. (2007). Stakeholder citizenship and transnational political participation: A normative evaluation of external voting. *Fordham Law Review*, *75*(5), 2393–2448 https://ir.lawnet.fordham.edu/flr/vol75/iss5/4.

Beckman, L. (2009). *The Frontiers of Democracy: The right to vote and its limits*. Palgrave Macmillan.

Beerbohm, E. (2016). The ethics of electioneering. *Journal of Political Philosophy*, *24*(4), 381–405. https://doi.org/10.1111/jopp.12082

Bentham, Jeremy. (1999). Essay on Political Tactics. In Michael James, Cyprian Blamires, & Catherine Pease Watkin (Eds.), *Political tactics*. Oxford: Clarendon Press (Original work published in 1843).

Bernal, V. (2010). Nationalist Networks: The eritrean diaspora online. In A. Alonso & P. Oiarzabal (Eds.), *Diasporas in the new media age: Identity, politics, and community* (pp. 122–135). University of Nevada Press.

Burke, E. (1996). Speech at the conclusion of the poll 3 November 1774. In W. M. Elofson, Woods, John A., Todd, William B. eds. (Ed.), *The writings and speeches of Edmund Burke. Vol. 3, Party, Parliament and the American War. 1774-1780* 3 . Oxford: Oxford University Press 63–70 http://dx.doi.org/10.1093/actrade/9780198224143.book.1 (Original work published in 1774) .

Caramani, D., & Grotz, F. (2015). Beyond citizenship and residence? Exploring the extension of voting rights in the age of globalization. *Democratization*, *22*(5), 799–819. https://doi.org/10.1080/13510347.2014.981668

Christiano, T. (2008). *The constitution of equality: Democratic authority and its limits*. Oxford University Press.

Cohen, J. (1989). Deliberation and democratic legitimacy. In P. H. Alan & P. Pettit (Eds.), *The good polity: Normative analysis of the State* (Oxford: Basil Blackwell) (pp. 17–34).

Collard, S., & Webb, P. (2020). UK parties abroad and expatriate voters: The Brexit Backlash. *Parliamentary Affairs*, *73*(4), 856–873. https://doi.org/10.1093/pa/gsaa040

Collyer, M. (2014). Inside out? Directly elected 'special representation' of emigrants in national legislatures and the role of popular sovereignty. *Political Geography*, *41*, 64–73. https://doi.org/10.1016/j.polgeo.2014.01.002

Collyer, M., & Vathi, Z. (2007). *Working Paper T22: Patterns of Extraterritorial Voting*. Department Research Centre on Migration, Globalisation, and Poverty. Retrieved August 27, 2019, from https://www.gov.uk/dfid-research-outputs/working-paper-t22-patterns-of-extraterritorial-voting#citation

Elgie, R. (2005). France: Stacking the Deck. In M. Gallagher & P. Mitchell (Eds.), *The Politics of Electoral Systems*. Oxford University Press 119–136 .

Forest, B., & Medeiros, M. (2020). Contiguity, constituencies, and the political representation of minorities. *Environment and Planning C: Politics and Space* 39 5 879–899 doi:https://doi.org/10.1177/2399654420972401 ,

Gauja, A. (2020). Temporarily' Abroad: Partisan organisation and mobilisation outside australia. *Parliamentary Affairs*, *73*(4), 874–886. https://doi.org/10.1093/pa/gsaa042

Gutmann, A., & Thompson, D. (2004). *Why deliberative democracy?* Princeton University Press.

Handley, L. (2008). A comparative survey of structures and criteria for boundary limitation. In L. Handley & B. Grofman (Eds.), *Redistricting in Comparative Perspective* (pp. 265–306). Oxford University Press.

Hopkin, J. (2005). Spain: Proportional representation with majoritarian outcomes. In M. Gallagher & P. Mitchell (Eds.), *The politics of electoral systems*. Oxford University Press 375–396 .

Hutcheson, D. S., & Arrighi, J.-T. (2015). "Keeping Pandora's (ballot) box half-shut": A comparative inquiry into the institutional limits of external voting in EU Member States. *Democratization*, *22*(5), 884–905. https://doi.org/10.1080/13510347.2014.979161

International Institute for Democracy and Electoral Assistance (IDEA). (2016). *Voting from Abroad Database*. (Retrieved September 17, 2020, from) https://www.idea.int/data-tools/data/voting-abroad

James, M. R. (2015). Two Concepts of Constituency. *The Journal of Politics*, *77*(2), 381–393. https://doi.org/10.1086/679494

Kalu, V., & Scarrow, S. E. (2020). US Parties Abroad: Partisan mobilising in a federal context. *Parliamentary Affairs*, *73*(4), 887–900. https://doi.org/10.1093/pa/gsaa043

Kolodny, N. (2014). Rule over None I: What justifies democracy? *Philosophy & Public Affairs*, *42*(3), 195–229. https://doi.org/10.1111/papa.12035

Landemore, H. (2012). Democratic Reason: The mechanisms of collective intelligence in politics. In H. Landemore & J. Elster (Eds.), *Collective Wisdom: Principles and mechanisms*. Cambridge University Press 251–289 .

Lopez-Guerra, C. (2005). Should Expatriates Vote? *Journal of Political Philosophy*, *13*(2), 216–234. https://doi.org/10.1111/j.1467-9760.2005.00221.x

Mansbridge, J. (2015). A minimalist definition of deliberation. In P. Heller & V. Rao (Eds.), *Deliberation and Development: Rethinking the role of voice and collective action in unequal societies*. World Bank 27–50 .

Mill, J. S. ([1861] 2008). *Considerations on representative government*. Electric Book Company.

Mitchell, P. (2005). The United Kingdom: Plurality Rule Under Siege. In M. Gallagher & P. Mitchell (Eds.), *The politics of electoral systems*. Oxford University Press 157–184 .

Owen, D. (2010). Resident aliens, non-resident citizens and voting rights. In G. Calder, C. Phillip, & J. Seglow (Eds.), *Citizenship acquisition and national belonging: Migration, membership and the liberal democratic state*. Palgrave Macmillan 52–73 .

Palop-García, P. (2018). Contained or represented? The varied consequences of reserved seats for emigrants in the legislatures of Ecuador and Colombia. *Comparative Migration Studies*, *6*(1 1–20). https://doi.org/10.1186/s40878-018-0101-7

Phillips, A. (1998). *The Politics of Presence*. Oxford University Press.

Pogonyi, S. (2014). Four patterns of non-resident voting rights. *Ethnopolitics*, *13*(2), 122–140. https://doi.org/10.1080/17449057.2013.846041

Rawls, J. (1973). *A Theory of Justice*. Oxford University Press.

Rehfeld, A. (2005). *The Concept of Constituency: Political representation, democratic legitimacy, and institutional design*. Cambridge University Press.

Rubio-Marin, R. (2006). Transnational politics and the democratic nation-state: Normative challenges of expatriate voting and nationality retention of emigrants. *New York University Law Review*, *81*(1), 117–147 https://www.nyulawreview.org/issues/volume-81-number-1/transnational-politics-and-the-democratic-nation-state-normative-challenges-of-expatriate-voting-and-nationality-retention-of-emigrants/.

Saalfeld, T. (2005). Germany: Stability and strategy in a mixed-member proportional system. In M. Gallagher & P. Mitchell (Eds.), *The politics of electoral systems*. Oxford University Press 209–230 .

Schwartz, N. L. (1988). *The blue guitar: Political representation and community*. University of Chicago Press.

Spiro, P. J. (2006). Perfecting political diaspora. *New York University Law Review*, *81*(1), 207–233 https://www.nyulawreview.org/issues/volume-81-number-1/perfecting-political-diaspora/.

Sunstein, C. R. (1991). Preferences and politics. *Philosophy & Public Affairs*, *20*(1), 3–34 http://www.jstor.org/stable/2265216.

Tager, M. (2006). Expatriates and Elections. *Diaspora: A Journal of Transnational Studies*, *15*(1), 35–60. https://doi.org/10.1353/dsp.0.0033

Thompson, D. F. (2002). *Just elections: Creating a fair electoral process in the United States*. University of Chicago Press.

Williams, M. (1998). *Voice, trust, and memory: Marginalized groups and the failings of liberal representation*. Princeton University Press.

Young, I. M. (1993). Justice and communicative democracy. In R. S. Gottlieb (Ed.), *Radical Philosophy: Tradition, counter-tradition, politics*. Temple University Press 123–143 .

Østergaard-Nielsen, E., & Ciornei, I. (2019). Making the absent present: Political parties and emigrant issues in country of origin parliaments. *Party Politics*, *25*(2), 153–166. https://doi.org/10.1177/1354068817697629

What's wrong with the presentist bias? On the threat of intergenerational domination

Anja Karnein

ABSTRACT
What is the wrong behind the widely criticized presentist bias of democracies? In this paper I argue that it is not that future generations are excluded from present-day democratic decision-making quite generally. Rather, I claim that due to the unique risks associated with representing future generations and the limitations on affecting future generations both institutionally and causally, the focus ought to be on including them on a more specific, narrower, set of issues, namely only those that threaten to lead to their domination. I identify such issues as those that may end up being purpose-determining: that may subject future generations to previous generations' will by forcing them to exert a substantial amount of their energies on dealing with problems caused by their predecessors. I conclude by reflecting on the extent to which political representation together with providing avenues of contestation can minimize the risk of intergenerational domination.

The presentist bias of democratic politics has become a widely recognized and much discussed topic. But what exactly is wrong with being politically short-sighted? Why can the present not trust that future generations will look out for themselves once their time comes? In this paper I show that, for the most part, the present can trust that the future will look out for itself. Since future generations will have full political sovereignty over their lives once they come into existence, they are in a different position from those lacking political voice today but who may be profoundly affected by the policy decisions of their contemporaries. The only chance at being heard for resident non-citizens, children or those with certain mental disabilities, for instance, is now, during their current life times. Future generations, by contrast, have their entire political lives ahead of them and can, at least in most cases, reorganize the world as it is left to them to their liking, even if this may sometimes be very costly.

This having been said, there are some issues that threaten to undermine the ability of future generations to have this kind of political say over their own lives. A present generation may, for instance, by being short-sighted, create a situation in which future generations are forced to design their lives around having to avert threats created by that present generation. On such occasions, I claim, the relationship degenerates from one between generations equally entitled to determine their purpose to one of intergenerational domination. It is with respect to such issues that the political inclusion of future generations is required. This is not because these are the only ways the present can wrong the future, but rather because they are the most serious.

The reason for not being more inclusive about the sorts of issue on which future generations ought to be presently included is that there are serious risks and costs associated with such inclusion, always involving the potential for error and abuse, thereby threatening to undermine the legitimacy of the democratic process among contemporary citizens. This risk is somewhat inevitable due to the special difficulties involved in representing those who do not yet exist and will not do so for the duration of their representation. I thus maintain that it is important to limit the representation of future generations to those instances in which their own chance of rectifying the wrongs of the past in a self-determined manner is at stake.

My argument proceeds in three steps. I begin by explaining why there are reasons to be cautious of a general inclusion of future generations, even if future generations seem to be entitled to such inclusion. I spell out both the inherent dangers to the democratic process among contemporaries such representation inevitably brings as well as the circumstance that, in many cases, future generations will get the chance to affirm or reverse decisions made earlier. Even if this is plausible, however, I demonstrate, second, that some ways a past generation can affect future generations may threaten the relational equality between the generations by potentially making one generation unacceptably beholden to another, thus leading to a form of intergenerational domination. I show that such domination is only in some central respects like intragenerational domination, but that it is domination nevertheless. In a third step I briefly spell out the implication of my analysis for the democratic inclusion of future generations. I suggest that, as in the intragenerational case, forms of political representation of future generations together with avenues of contestation constitute promising tools for limiting the risk of nondomination. My claims here are meant to provide a general outline of these institutional remedies, and not to constitute a full-fledged institutional proposal. The main aim of my argument is to reevaluate the end to which future generations ought to be included in current democratic decision-making and not primarily to assess the means of doing so.

I

Most scholars who worry about the presentist bias of democracies are concerned about the various ways short-sighted policies might either be less beneficial for the future than they could be or simply have detrimental future effects. With regard to the problematic consequences of climate change, for instance, Genevieve Fuji Johnson writes that they could '[all [. . .] be detrimental to the range of life options available in the present and in the future, possibly limiting movement, curbing productive choices, and reducing life expectancy.' (Johnson, 2007, p. 71) Andreas Bengtson goes further and claims that, if one is worried about not including those who may be affected by certain policy decisions, one ought not only include negative but also positive effects (Bengtson, 2021, regarding future generations see p. 719).

But both views are too wide. If future generations need to be included in all decisions that may impact them in some way, they will presumably have to be included in most current policy decisions, with very few exceptions. I want to resist this conclusion. This is not because I consider present generations to be entitled to affect the future in whatever way they wish. Nor is it because I think that there is something wrong, in principle, with including moral agents on all matters that affect them in some way (as proposed, for instance, by Goodin, 2007). Instead, it is because including future generations in present-day decision-making processes carries (1) inherent dangers to the democratic process among contemporaries. Moreover, (2) the way future generations are frequently affected by the actions or omissions of previous generations is quite different from the ways other affected but often disenfranchised groups are impacted, such as resident noncitizens, children, or those with certain mental disabilities. The ways in which the present can victimize – or empower – the future are much more limited and less straightforward, both (a) institutionally and (b) causally.

(1) The problems involved in representing future generations are manifold.[1] To begin with, there is no way for future generations to elect or appoint their representatives in the present. Similarly, there is no way for future generations to hold anyone accountable who purports to speak on their behalf. And there is no way for future generations to make sure that they are not being misrepresented, nor could they do anything about it if they were. This is connected to an inherent causal asymmetry between nonoverlapping generations: While the actions of the current generation may deeply affect future generations, nothing they do has any causal consequence for the present. They are not now capable of action, and presently have no will or judgment of their own.

In light of these problems, the danger of establishing representatives for future generations is that there is no way to ensure that debates about the interests of future generations do not end up centering on mere projections of contemporary (i.e. not future) citizens. This may happen as the result of more or less honest mistakes. A representative may sincerely think they are speaking on behalf of future generations but simply be projecting their own values on to the future. Such mistakes are easy enough to make since many things could be said to be in the interest of future generations. It is plausible to claim that future generations would want us to invest heavily in mitigating climate change, for instance. However, it is also plausible to claim that they would prefer that the present not spend its resources this way and let them deal with the problem when their time comes. After all, they might be able to do so with the help of the greater resources – presumably wealth – the non-mitigating present can leave to them. But representatives may also make less innocent mistakes. They could be genuinely insincere about what they hold the interests of future generations to be.

Either way, if representatives are wrong for whatever reason, they will, to the extent they have a say in contemporary democratic politics, risk undermining the power of contemporary citizens. While there may be ways to reduce the likelihood of such outcomes – as I describe in more detail in section III, by, for instance, including a large number of diverse viewpoints in the deliberation and subjecting any proposals to thorough debate in the public sphere – there is no real way to avoid them entirely if future generations are to be given an effective voice. Having an effective voice means either constituting part of the parliamentary votes or the ability to veto decisions. It does not mean being merely relegated to providing deliberative input. Thus, even if one considers future members of a society to be part of the demos, their representation is fraught in such a way that including them today has to be done with utmost care. But this may not be as worrisome as it sounds, given the various limitations to how one generation can affect another, to which I now turn.

(2) Much of what the present does or fails to do will affect the future in some, possibly profound, way. But the future has enough distance, temporally speaking, to be able to choose how to relate to these effects, that is, whether to accept or to reject them. This applies both to (a) institutional as well as (b) causal effects.

(a) A prominent and well-established way of worrying about the influence the present may exert on the future is institutional. Thomas Jefferson and Thomas Painefamously argued against being governed by the dead hand of the past (Jefferson 1999, pp. 593-598; Paine 1999, pp. 5-6). More recently, Dennis Thompson has expressed a similar concern, namely when he worries about the potential 'inter-temporal tyranny' that may result when constitutions are entrenched or, more generally, political constraints are rendered difficult to overcome (Thompson, 2005, pp. 247, 251).

The question is whether we view the difficulties involved in amending legal provisions as insurmountable shackles and thus, as highly suspect, or simply as the cost of change that accompanies the need for political stability as well as for the protection of minorities. Arguably, future generations will be able to do what they please with what previous generations bequeath to them. This is true even if some choices might be more difficult or costly to make given the previous generations' decisions on certain matters – such choices may, for instance, require a two-third majority to change a constitutional provision. But, as Ludwig Beckman points out: 'If future people wish to modify the laws passed down by us, they are of course free to do so. If future people do not modify these laws, this is presumably because they do not want to.' (Beckman, 2013, p. 781).[2]

Empirical research appears to bear out Beckman's claim. It seems, for instance, that most constitutions tend to go for specificity and flexibility rather than entrenchment (Versteeg & Zackin, 2016). And, although this is presumably part of the reason why constitutions are revised every 19 years in more than half of all democracies (Elkins et al., 2009), entrenched documents themselves need to be very flexible when it comes to textual interpretation if they are to stand the test of time. Again, claiming that there are serious limits to how much a previous generation can institutionally bind future generations is not to suggest that a previous generation may not make it costly for future generations to effect legal change (see also, Beckman, 2008, p. 614, 2013, p. 781). But there is surely no requirement to enable self-government at zero cost. This would be an impossible requirement. Even having to rewrite the constitution is costly, in some cases costlier than simply amending an existing one. Thus, there seems to be no costless way for generations to govern themselves. Viewed from this perspective, institutional precommitments seem far less objectionable.

(b) Unlike the pervasive effect any significant change may have on contemporaries, it seems that even very profound changes over generations can often be independently evaluated by future generations and either endorsed or neutralized in a way that may make it permissible to defer a hearing of their opinion to when they actually exist. Consider, for instance, the case of a community in the future whose groundwater has been contaminated by some unsustainable toxic waste disposal in the past. Assuming that this contamination is public knowledge, there are two paths the future community could take.

(i) *Costless*: because it would be expensive to clean the water or gain access to any other water source, members of the community end up drinking the water and getting sick.

(ii) *Costly*: the community heavily invests in providing clean drinking water. This is expensive but nobody ends up getting sick.

Choosing option (i) seems negligent, maybe even reckless, at least if there would have been a way for the community to pay for option (ii), and regardless of whether there was also wrongdoing on the part of the earlier generation(s) responsible for the toxic waste disposal. Option (ii) may seem historically unfair. It seems wrong for the future to have to shoulder the costs for what previous generations did. However, as long as there are ways to circumvent negative consequences due to past policy decisions from occurring, much of the onus of preventing detrimental effects of past actions in the future appears to lie in the future, historically unfair or not. To the extent this is plausible, it shows that there are clear limits to how future generations are necessarily victimized by the actions of previous generations, even those with profound(ly negative) impact. Future generations often have it in their power to stop this from happening, even if doing so may carry a steep price tag. This is in part because temporal distance provides a certain practical advantage: there will be more time for the detrimental effects of past generations' actions to surface, be publicly known and mitigated. But their ability to neutralize any damaging effects from the past is also, politically, due to future generations, as a collective, being sovereigns over their lives.[3] They have the political power and, in many cases, the material means, to decide which bequests of the past to accept and which to reject. Disenfranchised contemporary members of a society, such as resident noncitizens, children and people with certain mental disabilities, by contrast, do not have these two advantages: there is no temporal distance to shield them and they do not have any say in how the various decisions of their enfranchised contemporaries end up affecting them.[4]

To the extent it is compelling that future generations are less easily victimized by the actions or omissions of the presently living, the present appears to be entitled to take certain risks regarding the future – at least as long as they can be fairly certain that the future will be able to choose not to have the possible negative effects impact them. Just consider the beginning of industrialization, which, from the perspective of those who embarked upon it, clearly has had, and continues to have, highly perilous effects on the future. Had people then realized what we know now, namely the future dangers of climate change, should they not have engaged in it? The answer is not obvious. This is true especially had they also known, as we do now, that there was something we, today, could be doing about it, even if at great cost. It thus does not seem unreasonable to think that certain intergenerational risk- and cost- impositions may be justifiable.

This having been said, some developments are such that they do not merely produce negative but neutralizable effects on the quality of life of future persons. Instead, they may undermine the equal status of nonoverlapping generations, allowing previous generations to dominate following ones.

II

Thus far I have assumed that, whatever the past did, future generations can, possibly at some cost, choose to accept, reverse or change substantial parts thereof to their own liking. Arguably, some of the policies currently on the table, such as policies whose implications may aggravate climate change, do not 'simply' threaten to be costly to avoid. Rather, some policies with irreversible, detrimental, and long-term effects threaten to leave future generations to inherit a world that forces them to permanently exert most of their creative energies on trying to avoid disaster (Karnein, 2015, p. 64).[5] This, I now want to argue, is a highly inappropriate way of relating to future generations, amounting to a form of domination. The argument proceeds in three steps. I begin by explaining (1) why the concern ought to be about how we relate to future generations rather than about what ends up being distributed to them. I then (2) offer a definition of the kind of relational wrong involved – that of purpose-determination – and spell out its various parts. From here I go on to (3) defend the claim that intergenerational purpose-determination amounts to the wrong of intergenerational domination.

(1) Suppose climate change leads to extreme heatwaves (among very many other things, but let me focus on the heatwaves). In the worst case, future generations may be forced to live destitute lives or die. Let me call these scenarios SUFFERING and DEATH, respectively. To the extent such scenarios are avoidable, they clearly constitute impermissible bequests to the future. The question is what exactly renders them impermissible. There are at least two options: The dominant explanation in the literature is that what makes SUFFERING and DEATH wrong is a radical lowering of the quality of life that developments such as extreme heatwaves will bring – either comparatively (rendering future generations worse off than we are ourselves, see, Mazor, 2010), hypothetically (rendering them worse off than we would want to be left off, see, Rawls, 1971) or absolutely (making them fall below a certain threshold, see, Meyer & Roser, 2009). Thinking about the wrong involved in SUFFERING and DEATH this way, however, leaves nothing to say about the following case: Consider a very wealthy future, one where not just enough was left to the future, or as much as the previous generations had, but much more. In this scenario, therefore, all just mentioned distributive desiderata – enough, same or more – have been achieved. Assume, however, that members of this future live under the constant threat of disaster they have to devote their lives to trying to avoid. The problem here does not primarily have something to do with a lack of having resources. Rather, the chief problem is that those affected, presumably one or more generations, have to make it their purpose to find ways and means to remedy the detrimental consequences of past generations' actions or omission in order to avoid SUFFERING and DEATH or the prospect of both.[6] Let me call this case

WEALTHY IN CHAINS. There is something seriously wrong in WEALTHY IN CHAINS, and this something cannot be captured by theories of intergenerational justice that follow the distributive paradigm.[7]

Instead, and this is the second, less obvious, option for understanding the wrong involved in SUFFERING and DEATH, the problem lies in the way past generations relate to future generations in these cases. WEALTHY IN CHAINS, but also SUFFERING and DEATH, are wrong because they violate the relational equality between the generations.

(2) In WEALTHY IN CHAINS the relational equality between the generations is violated because one generation ends up imposing its will on another by largely determining the latter's purpose.[8] Having one's purpose determined in this way implies a scenario in which future generations are confronted with developments,

(a) initiated by previous generations in an intentional, reckless or negligent manner
(b) that, in order not to lead to SUFFERING or DEATH,
(c) require one or more generations to comprehensively
(d) and continuously direct their energies toward averting these outcomes

Let me spell out these different features in more detail.

(a) If a generation were to end up having its purpose determined by some non-anthropological natural disaster or even by a completely innocent previous generation (perhaps the purpose-determining development is the result of a sincere accident nobody could have foreseen) this would be very unfortunate, but no wrong would be involved. If future generations have no reason to resent the attitudes toward themselves, manifested in the developments they are forced to exert their energies to trying to avoid, it is not an intersubjective relationship that is at stake.

(b) If the development at issue is one future generations would prefer to avoid but without there being an existential threat – perhaps a future generation would prefer not to have inherited a deeply engrained commitment to capitalistic values that will be next to impossible to shake during its tenure on earth – then this, again, would be unfortunate, but it would not necessarily amount to purpose-determination. This is because it is not inconceivable to live with these undesirable but not life-threatening values without exerting a lot of energy trying to undo them.

(c) Some detrimental developments that may be costly and keep a generation occupied in various respects will not amount to being purpose-determining since they will not require a comprehensive response. Consider the early days of climate change, when slowly reducing the use of fossil and transitioning to new energy sources might have sufficed to get the problem under control. This would have required some costly transitions, including, perhaps, some life-style changes, but not much beyond that. Compare this to what it increasingly looks like now, where contemporary inaction makes a future likely with a radically destabilized climate. In this future everyone may have to be focused on avoiding disaster in an all-encompassing manner, that is, in their reproductive-, career-, leisure time- and consumer choices: they will have to carefully consider whether their reproductive choices are sustainable or ethically justifiable to the offspring, careers will have to increasingly be geared at overcoming the central problems connected to extreme weather, leisure activities will need to be scrutinized according to their safety and sustainability under smoldering temperatures, and consumer choices will have to reflect both an awareness that the problem may not be perpetuated as well as a response to the current situation. This would thus amount to a generation having to comprehensively direct its energies to trying to avert disaster.[9]

(d) Similarly, the difference between a future scenario that 'merely' imposes costs on a future generation and one that determines its purpose is that, in the former case, no matter how extensive the required activities may be, they are also likely to be clearly delineated: in the early days of climate change, for instance, a certain degree of pollution would have needed to be avoided or mitigated and a certain amount of infrastructural changes would have needed to be made to adapt to some of the detrimental consequences of climate change the world is committed to. Purpose-determination, by contrast, requires that the threat a generation is forced to avert is continuous or, as I will discuss in section (3c) below in more detail, reverberating, with no clearly delineated boundaries to the efforts required. This having been said, while a certain temporal extent of the problem is required, the exact degree of this extent may differ: determining a generation's purpose for ten years, say, is continuous and thus problematic, but the situation would be aggravated in a case in which a development is such that no end is in sight: where, no matter how much a generation tries, the fetters that hold them keep holding or, short of that, keep reappearing.

In sum, there might be situations that are costly and quite occupying for future generations for a significant amount of time, without however, being serious or comprehensive enough or sufficiently temporally extended to amount to what may be called purpose determining. Identifying precisely where developments that are 'merely' costly end and those that are purpose-determining begin will be a contested issue. But even though there might be some grey areas I believe that the distinction is normatively crucial. In what follows I will try to shed some more light on the four conditions, all of which I take to be necessary and jointly sufficient for intergenerational domination.

(3) Suppose this account of purpose-determination is plausible. Can it really amount to what might be called intergenerational domination? There are two sorts of doubts one may have about this. The first is that domination is not the sort of wrong that can occur between nonoverlapping generations. The second is that, even if there is such a thing as intergenerational domination, my account of purpose-determination does not amount to something that can be called domination, most prominently perhaps, because it seems to be overly concerned with the type of effects certain interactions might cause as opposed to the interactions themselves. In what follows I (a) briefly introduce Philip Pettit's definition of domination and show how, on a superficial reading of it, it seems apparent that one generation can dominate another. I show how some authors have picked up on this in order to apply the notion intergenerationally. From here I go on to (b) demonstrate that, on closer inspection, there are some important disanalogies between how domination applies intra- and intergenerationally. These have been helpfully pointed out by Beckman and so I critically discuss his objections to the idea that climate change, for instance, could ever constitute a case of intergenerational domination. I argue, against Beckman, that while the cases indeed differ in some respects, enough of the core idea of domination can be applied intergenerationally to make sense of certain impermissible asymmetries between nonoverlapping generations. In this context I also argue that the way the cases differ explains how my account of intergenerational purpose-determination amounts to domination: given that previous generations will always have left the scene by the time the future arrives, a capacity to interfere will have a lot to do with the particular kinds of developments in question and how these impact those currently alive (this is not unlike the case among contemporaries where interferences with negligible impact would also not count as domination).

(a) According to Pettit's definition, 'one agent dominates another if and only if they have a certain power over that other, in particular a power of interference on an arbitrary basis' (Pettit, 1997, p. 52). On a cursory look at this definition, the current generation clearly has the power to causally affect the future – negatively and positively – in an arbitrary way, that is, in a way that does not track the interests of future generations,[10] with nothing the future can do about it. Thus, John Nolt, for instance, claims that it is clear that when we negatively affect the future, such as, for instance, in the case of climate change, 'we (...) are by our emissions of greenhouse gases dominators of posterity' (Nolt 2011, 62).[11] Patrick Taylor Smith has rightly objected that the concerns about domination cannot be limited to cases of actual interference or harm, but that the mere power or ability of the present to negatively affect future generations already renders intergenerational relationships inherently dominating, whether the present acts on this ability or not (Smith, 2013, p. 226).

This seems right: possessing this power suffices. But, and here my view parts with that of Smith, while all generations can be profoundly impacted by what their predecessors do or fail to do, only some face the threat of having their purpose determined. It is the capacity to produce these effects that needs to be avoided in the name of nondomination, not 'simply' the prospect of costly mitigation, or so I am claiming.[12]

(b) Invoking domination in the intergenerational sphere this way is, however, controversial. On closer inspection, several disanalogies between intra- and intergenerational domination become apparent. Beckman, who is among the few who have systematically scrutinized this issue, points out three. The first is that domination must involve the capacity to make arbitrary choices for another party, which is not given between parties removed in time. The second is that domination requires physical proximity, which is also not possible between nonoverlapping generations. The third is that domination entails a kind of intentionality that is often absent intergenerationally. Let me discuss each of these aspects in turn.

According to Beckman, future generations are never subject to the capacity of previous generations to choose between various options, since the time lapse ensures that whatever decisions the past made have materialized by the time future generations enter the scene (2016, 293–4). In other words, there is nothing the past can do once the future comes into existence. No living person can be subject to the current arbitrary decisions of a dead person. Let me illustrate this with the following two cases, the first intra- and the second intergenerational:

> (i)Intra*generational*. A rents an apartment from B. There is no renter-protection so A is entirely subject to B's arbitrary will. B could, for instance, simply decide to enter one night, remove kitchen and bathroom and demolish the walls.
>
> (ii)*Intergenerational*. A inherits an apartment from B, now deceased. While alive, B removed the kitchen and bathroom and demolished the walls.

Unlike in (i), the intragenerational case, in (ii), the intergenerational case, A need not worry that B drops by unexpectedly to render the apartment unlivable. A simply finds it that way. And Pettit indeed claims that it is an important feature of institutions geared at ensuring non-domination that they avoid the psychological toll that accompanies (i). 'To suffer the reality or expectation of arbitrary interference [...] is to have to endure a high level of uncertainty, since the arbitrary basis on which the interference occurs means that there is no predicting when it will strike. Such uncertainty makes planning [...] difficult. [...] And, of course, it is also likely to produce a high level of anxiety' (Pettit, 1997, p. 85). But while uncertainty and the associated anxiety may be something the ideal of non-domination can avoid, it could still be the case that instances in which there is no uncertainty and no anxiety are also ones of domination. As Frank Lovett argues, the slave who learns to predict her master's behaviors is no less dominated than a slave who is constantly surprised by it (Lovett, 2012, p. 138).

Still, Beckman might reply, it remains true that, whatever interference by past generations future generations may have to live with, the latter are never subject to the continued, or active, capacity to interfere by the former: the interference will have occurred or it will have not. The appliances will be there or they will be gone – nobody will be coming to get them at some random point.

While it is true that future generations need not fear any active interference, and that this is a substantial difference to the intragenerational case, there is a kind of interference that has continuous effects, like an echo that may continue to be 'active' long after its source has become silent. Just consider the following version of my above illustration:

> (i')Intra*generational*. A rents an apartment from B. There is no renter-protection so A is entirely subject to B's arbitrary will. B regularly releases mice into the apartment.
>
> (ii')*Intergenerational*. A inherits an apartment from B, now deceased. While alive, B lets mice inhabit the space.

Here, even in the intergenerational case, while B is gone for good, it is quite possible that, whatever A does, the mice will keep coming back at random intervals. Similarly, a generation may continually suffer from the effects of past generations' interferences. This may be the case, for instance, if the heatwaves the past is responsible for keep coming and need constant attention in order to avoid fatalities. In this case, it is not unreasonable to assume that the heatwaves will be perceived by their victims as a danger that continues to emanate (condition (d) of what renders a development purpose-determining), in unpredictable forms, from the reckless or negligent choices of past generations (condition (a) of what renders a development purpose-determining). The same applies if, more generally, the climate change past generations failed to aggressively mitigate keeps wreaking new and surprising havoc on the future. This, I want to suggest, constitutes something very similar to the continual capacity to interfere, namely the capacity to interfere that has a continual effect.

A critic may point out that there is still a difference: the past may be continually interfering with the future, but in ways it never had foreseen and cannot, in that future, control. Presumably, in the intragenerational case, the dominating party knows what she is doing and can control her actions. But it is unclear how important continued control actually is. Just imagine a situation in which the dominating party has gone mad. Her actual interferences thus no longer are expressions of her active moral agency. But still, her capacity to interfere will not cease to amount to domination just because she has no real control over it. This is because the structure that puts or leaves her in her asymmetrically powerful position is the problem. And the same holds true intergenerationally: under certain circumstances and regarding particular kinds of issues, former generations have the capacity to initiate perpetual, random, interferences the future has to continually deal with somehow: as suggested above, at some point, if the present continues to fail to mitigate climate change, detrimental effects will be such that they randomly, but constantly, interfere with, and direct, people's lives.

This having been said, there is certainly something that remains of the disanalogy Beckman calls attention to. Since future persons find themselves in a world that has been left to them in a certain way, the degree to which their lives are subjected to any particular case of power assertion by previous generations may be significantly unlike the way a person or group is subjected to the seemingly same form of power assertion by a contemporary. While the problem in the intragenerational case is the continual capacity to interfere, the problem in the intergenerational case is the capacity to interfere in a way that reverberates continually. Whereas the continual capacity is always present if social structures enable this, the capacity to interfere in a way that reverberates continually will be limited to certain sorts of interferences, namely those that threaten to play out this way. In the intergenerational case it, therefore, can only be certain instances of a previous generation's capacity for arbitrary power assertion that threaten domination – namely those that threaten to become purpose determining.

But there are further disanalogies. Beckman proceeds by noting that for the intragenerational case, one of the markers of domination is that one party – the dominated – acts with deference to the other – dominating – party. And, indeed, Pettit writes that '[the dominated, strategy-bound person is someone with reason to watch what they say, someone who must be assumed always to have an eye to what will please their dominators' (Pettit, 1997, p. 91). But future generations cannot act with deference toward their ancestors, since that requires contemporaneity (Beckman, 2016, p. 295). It is certainly true that members of nonoverlapping generations never actually meet, making the physical experience of not being able to look the other in the eye impossible. But it is entirely conceivable that an earlier generation feels superior to a later generation or, at least, indifferent to it. More importantly even, and as alluded to in the context of spelling out condition (a) of what makes a development purpose-determining, it is easy to imagine that a later generation feels disrespected by the acts or omissions of a previous generation and possibly resentment towards it. Such resentment is less likely and, more significantly, also less appropriate, if a generation 'merely' has to make costly changes or adjustments to what was left to them by the past. But resentment is entirely in order if a substantial part of a generation's options and choices bear the mark of recklessness or negligence by former generations.

The final disanalogy Beckman mentions has to do with intentionality. Arguably, standard intragenerational forms of domination must involve an intention to interfere (Pettit, 1997, p. 53), which Beckman claims will often be lacking in the intergenerational case. Although he admits that it is not impossible that one generation can intentionally interfere with another, Beckman suggests that, when it comes to a case such as climate change, for instance, there is really no direct intention to interfere with the future. Rather, any actual interference that occurs is an unintended byproduct of otherwise, or individually, oftentimes benign activities. 'Hence, the people hurt by climate change are not subject to domination because they are not the victims of the intended attempt by the emitters of greenhouse gases to make others conform to their will' (Beckman, 2016, p. 296).

One might generalize this point. Even if it is possible for one generation to intentionally leave undesirable bequests to future generations, it will often be the case that any negative interference that occurs by one generation on the next is not, itself, intentional. Rather, it is the unintended byproduct of actions or omissions that a generation intends to pursue. But even if one generation does not usually intend to wrong another, for the required intentionality to hold it suffices that one generation knows and thus accepts negative consequences as a result of otherwise – let us assume – benign pursuits. This amounts to negligence and, as such, is included in Pettit's original definition. '[T]he worsening that interference involves always has to be more or less intentional in character: it cannot occur by accident, for example, as when I fall in your path or happen to compete with you for scarce goods; it must be at least the sort of action in the doing of which we can sensibly allege negligence' (Pettit, 1997, p. 52). In other words, I agree with Beckman that presumably no generation intends for climate change to end up dominating the future. But, in contrast to Beckman, I am suggesting that implicitly accepting both the negative consequences and that these might lead to a situation in which future generations have their purpose determined, constitutes a sufficient amount of intentionality to clearly distinguish the case of anthropological climate change from a genuinely natural catastrophe having similar effects on future generations.

Thus, while the details may differ, enough of the core idea of domination, namely that one party has the ability to interfere with another arbitrarily, thereby subjecting the other to their will (as opposed to tracking the interests of the other), holds between nonoverlapping generations, at least under certain circumstances. These circumstances are those I identify as purpose-determining. Under this threshold any arbitrary interference fails to undermine the equal status of future generations since, unlike in the intragenerational case, the interference is then not potent enough to amount to what may be described as subjecting the other to one's will. B

III

If, as I am proposing, the wrong behind the presentist bias is that it may lead to intergenerational domination, one might think that the remedy is clear: as in the intragenerational case, what is required for preventing domination is both political representation of future generations as well as the provision of avenues of contestation. In what follows I briefly reflect on (a) what, in broad strokes, such representation may look like and on (b) what dangers of domination remain and ought to be addressed via contestatory means. I discuss two such dangers, that of future generations being relegated to 'sticky' minorities in current democratic decision-making, and that of representatives who may be mistaken about the interests of future generations.

(a) As already mentioned, future generations can neither authorize anyone to represent them nor hold anyone accountable. But this does not mean that there can be no criteria for representing future generations. There are at least two aspects of such representation one can apply normative criteria to, both of which play a role in setting it up as an institution and judging its performance. These are, first, the principles on the basis of which a representative makes decisions for future generations and, second, the procedural mechanisms by which a representative comes to deliberate and interpret what the principles mean in any particular case (which also include some further specifications of who would be a good representative).

With regard to the principles, the account I am offering suggests that representatives have one primary such principle, which is to ensure treatment of future generations as worthy of equal respect and as equally entitled to exercise sovereignty over their collective lives. The guiding principle is, in other words, to avoid intergenerational domination. Once future generations' interests are effectively included in contemporary decision-making with regard to those policy issues that threaten to have reverberating effects, certain gambles by the present may be justified. Such gambles may include ones that promise great benefits for the present at a level of risk for future generations that, after careful deliberation, representatives for future generations deem acceptable. Risks may be deemed acceptable either because the potential benefits for the future are also great or because the risks of such reverberating effects are very low.[13]

The main idea behind effective representation, however, is that by making our decisions today depend on the expected agreeability to the future, the decisions cease to be dominating – even if they end up having the reverberating effects I described earlier. As I already pointed out, for a relationship to be marked as dominating it is not enough for one party – the potentially dominated one – to suffer under certain circumstances. It is important that those circumstances are the result of the intentional, reckless or negligent behavior of former generations.

With regard to the procedures, the best way to ensure that the representatives genuinely consider the interests of future generations – and not simply their own interests disguised as those of future generations – is to include large and diverse numbers into the deliberations including both experts and nonexperts. This is also supported by the circumstance that these representatives' constituency is itself a large and diverse group. Ideally, this debate would be transparent and widely accessible so that it can itself be scrutinized by a public increasingly attuned to its intergenerational responsibilities. The larger the group of contemporaries critically debating the implications of some of their policies on the future, the more the risks and costs of representing future generations can be diminished.

But this seems to bring us full circle: what could a large number of contemporaries biased toward the present help? Presumably, the virtue of large numbers is that the presentist bias will be held to different degrees by different participants of the debate so that the deliberative group can check itself (see also, Smith, 2013, p. 241). More importantly, however, the bias itself, real as it currently is, may be based more on a misunderstanding that can be cleared up upon reflection rather than a deeply held view. Just recall the discussion of Beckman's claims earlier, especially where he points out, albeit indirectly, that it is not clear that the present would ever intentionally want to wrong the future. At its worst, therefore, one might think that the present accepts wronging as an unintended side-effect of its self-interested actions, at least as long as these side-effects are not clearly pointed out.

A further procedural point has to do with the powers vested in the representation of future generations. Some have suggested limiting such powers to restrict any threat the institution may pose to the power of present-day citizens to determine their own fate (Beckman & Uggla, 2017). The problem with this, however, is that such representation, lacking in any real political power, will do little to reign in instances of intergenerational domination. Thus, what is needed is representation with some political weight. While this indeed threatens to aggravate the risk of undermining the democratic powers of present-day citizens, the only way around this seems to be to restrict the issues on which future generations are included, which is one of the main proposals of the present paper. In addition, one has to make very sure that the representatives are forced to do all they can to ascertain the genuine interests of future generations regarding their independence from previous generations' will-imposition, both via some of the means already mentioned as well as via the avenues for contestation to which I now turn.

(b) For Pettit, avenues of contestation are as important as representation to combat domination. This is because the mere representation of minorities will frequently not be an effective means of preventing a majority from more or less arbitrarily imposing its will (Pettit, 1999, p. 178, 2012, pp. 211–213). In a certain way, even robust representation of future generations is likely to make their voices into no more than sticky minorities in contemporary democratic decisions.[14] This is for the opposite reason from what makes minorities sticky in the intragenerational context: unlike it is with contemporary minorities, if the numbers of future generations would be adequately represented, they would clearly be in the vast majority. Including them but, at the same time, keeping their numbers down, is thus highly artificial, albeit necessary: if one did not keep their numbers down, future generations would come to dominate present-day democratic processes and the sticky minorities would be the comparatively tiny group of all the currently living. Since this seems unacceptable, future generations, if included in present-day democratic decision-making, will not only be inadequately represented in terms of their numbers, but will also systematically be in the position of a sticky minority. Thus, the need for avenues of contestation may be as great, if not greater, in the intergenerational case as it is in the intragenerational case. What is more, in the intergenerational case there is the already mentioned further danger that representatives misconceive future generations' interests. In sum, the problem is twofold: future generations will be systematically under- and, possibly, mis-represented.

So what kind of avenues of contestation may be available to counteract these problems? For the intragenerational case, the solution Pettit proposes is 'a procedure that would enable people, not to veto public decisions on the basis of their avowable, perceived, interests, but to call them into question on such a basis and to trigger a review' (Pettit, 1999, p. 179). And since systems of individualized contestation are likely to create 'a build-up and backlog of endless complaints' (Pettit, 2012, p. 217), Pettit suggests establishing 'standardized ways of dealing with different types of issues where people's equal access to influence is generally agreed to be in danger' (ibid.). These standardized ways may include creating individual rights to protect against decision-making by the majority. The idea of creating individual rights, of course, is difficult to implement in a situation where the goal is to avoid the domination of future generations, since it is unclear which rights would tend to protect this sort of interest. The right to health, physical safety and a nontoxic environment may come to mind. But while these rights may protect against SUFFERING and DEATH, they may not do enough to protect against WEALTHY IN CHAINS. One right that may, indeed, go some way to protect against

WEALTHY IN CHAINS, which is collective, not individual, may be the right of peoples – or future generations, in this case – to self-determination. Establishing such a right would indeed be helpful if it could be invoked to contest decisions made by both representatives for future generations as well as those made by the majority as undermining or not doing enough to protect the interests of future generations.

Especially the possibility of misrepresentation highlights that trying to insure nondomination for future generations is a bit more complex than this already difficult task is in the context of contemporaries. Since, again, future persons are not around to verify what their representatives do or say in their name, there needs to be a way to scrutinize the representatives themselves. Here, as just suggested, establishing certain legal or even constitutional protections for future generations would hopefully prove to be useful, but someone has to make it their calling to actually contest. The proposals I offer above in the context of procedures will hopefully go some way to ameliorate this problem, namely to have both a large and diverse body of representatives as well as empowering members of the general public to question the sorts of interests of future generations identified by those claiming to represent them. All of this, however, relies on a public willing to engage in such deliberations and forms of contestation. In the intergenerational context it is thus vital not just to have a resistance-prone citizenry (Pettit, 2012, p. 220) but also a citizenry concerned with its obligations to future generations.

Thus, the gap between our institutional attempts at minimizing domination and the potential for domination that already characterizes constitutional democracies today may necessarily be even wider in the intergenerational case. But this seems to be the unavoidable consequences of the inherent asymmetry between the generations. A theory that highlights the dangers of domination cannot do more than attempt to do as much as possible to forestall opportunities for domination. If the current generation does all it can to reduce the capacity to arbitrarily cause reverberating effects that end up determining the purpose of future generations, it will have satisfied its intergenerational duty of justice, understood as the duty of nondomination.

IV

In this paper I have identified domination as the primary threat that renders the presentist bias of democracies troubling. Not all ways of relating to future generations are potentially dominating, and thus future generations ought to be included in the democratic process, via representation and appropriate avenues for contestation, only on a fairly narrow set of issues. While this may seem controversial, I am claiming that it is desirable given that the representation of future generations is riddled with difficulties and, if not designed carefully, may lead to domination of present citizens by the alleged interests of future generations.

Notes

1. The following section is an abbreviated version of arguments made in (Karnein, 2017), section 2.
2. One might be skeptical about the notion that not changing laws indicates that 'the future' does not want to do so – the 'future' is, after all, not a monolithic entity. But it is not unreasonable to assume that if the laws passed down by the previous generations are indeed highly problematic or otherwise unsuitable to the next generation, a supermajority should be achievable by those subjected (although it obviously depends on the supermajority required: nine tenths are much more difficult to accomplish than two thirds).
3. Jefferson captures this particular thought well when he writes that 'one generation is to another as one independent nation to another' (Jefferson, 1999, p. 596) .
4. None of this is to say that the way enfranchised members of one generation can affect contemporaries and future generations is necessarily different – contaminated water can, in principle, affect contemporaries just like it can affect future generations. I am simply suggesting that there will often be a difference in the way the recipients of these effects end up being impacted: while it is more likely that contemporaries end up being victimized, a lot has to go wrong for future generations to be victimized in the same way.
5. Note that the damage that has to occur before the threshold is reached may be substantial.
6. Should there be nothing for anyone to do but suffer or die, the wrong in question would be the same in principle, albeit 'on steroids,' since not only the choices and options would largely be determined by previous generations, but a whole generation's and perhaps humanity's fate and future.
7. Rainer Forst suggests that understanding justice as a primarily distributive paradigm is always mistaken (see, Forst, 2014, 2020). For a critique of this 'monistic' and an embrace of a more plural view of justice see, (Caney, 2014, p. 152.)
8. SUFFERING and DEATH are instances of purpose-determination in that I am assuming they are the result of a morally blamable action by previous generations (condition a), that generations so afflicted will do all they can, even if there is little chance of success, to avoid their fates in the two scenarios (condition b), and that his involves efforts which comprehensively (condition c) and continuously demand their attention (condition c).
9. For some cases it might be difficult to determine exactly they are 'merely' costly or purpose-determining. Consider a generation bereft of all infrastructure due to their predecessor's war activities (I am grateful to an anonymous reviewer for suggesting this example.) While this development may end up this way, it need not necessarily be purpose-determining: in principle, at least, the post-war generation is free to rebuild its physical structures as it sees fit and also free

in many other respects. This having been said, a previous generation's war may, indeed, become purpose-determining if, for instance, it causes trauma that continues to hold individuals or groups captive for the remainder of their lives.

10. (Pettit, 1997), 55. In more recent renditions, Pettit considers arbitrary those ways of interference that cannot be contested 2008, 109.
11. Actually, Nolt thinks that simply by virtue of being in an asymmetrical relationship with future generations, is the present generation dominating (61). But, or so he claims, it is not domination as such we ought to be concerned about. Rather, we should worry about domination that leads to harm. This is puzzling. It seems that on this account we might as well simply be concerned with harming future generations, especially given that intergenerational domination as such seems inescapable according to Nolt.
12. This focus could be established in two different ways. First, one can claim, with Smith, that all intergenerational relationships are marked by different degrees of domination. Then, unlike Smith, one might hold that only the more severe forms ought to be avoided. Second, one can distinguish between the ability to negatively impact the future – which does not amount to domination – and the ability to dominate, a qualitatively different kind of wrong. This is what I am trying to do.
13. I thank an anonymous reviewer for pressing me on this issue.
14. Pettit calls minorities 'sticky,' in cases where its members 'are independently identified individuals who, on certain issues, are more or less bound to be on the losing side' (Pettit, 2012, p. 212). What independently identifies future generations is that they are of the future: they do not currently exist and thus cannot speak for themselves.

Acknowledgments

I wish to thank Mattias Iser for his insightful comments on various drafts of this paper and many helpful discussions, as well as two anonymous reviewers for this journal and the editors of this special issue. I am also grateful for the stimulating questions of the organizers and participants of the conference "Participation for the long-term: ideas, individuals, institutions" held at the University of Turku, Finland, in December 2021, especially Henry Vogt and my commentator there, Simo Kyllönen.

Disclosure statement

No potential conflict of interest was reported by the author(s).

References

Beckman, L. (2008). Democratic inclusion, law, and causes. *Ratio Juris, 21*(3), 348–364. https://doi.org/10.1111/j.1467-9337.2008.00394.x

Beckman, L. (2013). Democracy and future generations: Should the unborn have a voice? In J. C. Merle (Ed.), *Spheres of global justice: Volume 2 fair distribution-global economic, social and intergenerational justice* (pp. 775–788). Springer.

Beckman, L. (2016). Power and Future People's Freedom: Intergenerational Domination, Climate Change, and Constitutionalism. *Journal of Political Power, 9* (2), 289–307. https://doi.org/10.1080/2158379X.2016.1191159

Beckman, L., & Uggla, F. (2017). The Ombudsman for Future Generations: Legitimate and Effective? In I. Gonzalez-Ricoy & A. Gosseries (Eds.), *Institutions for Future Generations* (pp. 117–134). Oxford University Press.

Bengtson, A. (2021). The All-Affected Principle and the Question of Asymmetry. *Political Research Quarterly, 74*(3), 718–728. https://doi.org/10.1177/1065912920938142

Caney, S. (2014). Justice and the Basic Right to Justification. In D. Owen (Ed.), *Justice, Democracy and the Right to Justification: Rainer Forst in Dialogue* (pp. 147–166). Bloomsbury Academic.

Elkins, Z., Ginsburg, T., & Melton, J. (2009). *The Endurance of National Constitutions*. Cambridge University Press.

Forst, R. (2014). *Justification and Critique* (pp. 17–37). Polity Press.

Forst, R. (2020). The Point of Justice. On the Paradigmatic Incompatibility between Rawlsian 'Justice as Fairness' and Luck Egalitarianism. In J. Mandle & S. Roberts-Cady (Eds.), *John Rawls: Debating the Major Questions*. Oxford University Press 148–160 .

Goodin, R. (2007). Enfranchising all affected interests, and its alternatives. *Philosophy & Public Affairs, 35*(1), 40–68. https://doi.org/10.1111/j.1088-4963.2007.00098.x

Jefferson, T. (1999). *Jefferson: Political Writings*. J. Appleby & T. Ball. Cambridge University Press.

Johnson, G. F. (2007). Discursive Democracy in the Transgenerational Context and a Precautionary Turn in Public Reasoning. *Contemporary Political Theory, 6*(1), 67–85. https://doi.org/10.1057/palgrave.cpt.9300253

Karnein, A. (2015). Climate Change and Justice Between Nonoverlapping Future Generations. *Global Justice: Theory Practice Rhetoric, 8*(2), 43–65. https://doi.org/10.21248/gjn.8.2.87

Karnein, A. (2017). Can we represent future generations? In A. Gosseries & I. Gonzalez-Ricoy (Eds.), *Institutions for Future Generations* (pp. 83–97). Oxford University Press.

Lovett, F. (2012). What Counts as Arbitrary Power? *Journal of Political Power, 5*(1), 137–152. https://doi.org/10.1080/2158379X.2012.660026

Mazor, J. (2010). Liberal Justice, Future People, and Natural Resource Conservation. *Philosophy & Public Affairs, 38*(4), 380–408. https://doi.org/10.1111/j.1088-4963.2010.01189.x

Meyer, L., & Roser, D. (2009). Enough for the Future. In A. Gosseries & L. Meyer (Eds.), *Intergenerational Justice* (pp. 219–248). Oxford University Press.

Nolt, J. (2011). Greenhouse Gas Emission and the Domination of Posterity. In D. Arnold (Ed.), *The Ethics of Global Climate Change*. Cambridge University Press.

Paine, T. (1999). *Rights of Man* Dover Publications, Inc. Original work published 1791.

Pettit, P. (1997). *Republicanism: A Theory of Freedom and Government*. Clarendon Press.

Pettit, P. (1999). Republican Freedom and Contestatory Democratization. In (D. Value, I. Shapiro, & C. Hacker-Cordon (Eds.), *Democracy's Value*. 163–190. Cambridge University Press.

Pettit, P. (2012). *On the People's Terms. A Republican Theory and Model of Democracy*. Cambridge University Press.

Rawls, J. (1971). *A Theory of Justice*. Harvard University Press.

Smith, P. T. (2013). The Intergenerational Storm: Dilemma or Domination. *Philosophy and Public Issues (New Series)*, *3*(1), 207–244.

Thompson, D. (2005). Democracy in Time: Popular Sovereignty and Temporal Representation. *Constellations*, *12*(2), 245–261. https://doi.org/10.1111/j.1351-0487.2005.00414.x

Versteeg, M., & Zackin, E. (2016). Constitutions Unentrenched: Toward an Alternative Theory of Constitutional Design. *American Political Science Review*, *110*(4), 657–674. https://doi.org/10.1017/S0003055416000447

Representing non-citizens: A proposal for the inclusion of all affected interests

Benjamin Boudou

ABSTRACT
This article defends the normative relevance of the representation of non-citizens in democracies. I argue that representation within nation-states constitutes a realistic institutionalisation of the All-Affected Principle, allowing justificatory practices towards non-citizens and establishing political institutions that can realise the ideal of inclusion of all externally affected individuals. I defend electoral, non-electoral and surrogate forms of representation of affected interests that satisfy both the cosmopolitan concern for the equal consideration of interests and the statist defence of the importance of a territorially and civically bounded demos. I assess piecemeal implementations of representation practices, namely reciprocal representation, ombudspersons, self-appointed representatives and deliberative and advocacy groups. Gradual and pluralised means of representation constitute necessary and feasible first steps to consider affected interests and offer an alternative route to an all-or-nothing defence of inclusion as national enfranchisement.

Introduction

This article defends the representation of non-citizens as a practical form of due consideration of their interests and a second-best alternative to their inclusion in the demos. I aim to justify different forms of representation of people who are not citizens of a given state but whose interests are nonetheless affected by the state's decisions. This category of 'non-citizens' is intentionally broad but mainly understood in a migration context; it includes foreign residents, immigrants with or without legal status, asylum seekers and refugees. Non-citizens face the following challenge: migration policies generate externalities for non-citizens, i.e. affect their interests and the fulfilment of their fundamental needs. For these policies to be legitimate, it has been argued that those who are affected should be included in the demos (Goodin, 2007) or that the externalities generated by the policies should be justified to those they constrain via cosmopolitan democratic institutions (Abizadeh, 2008).

I wish to narrow my focus by examining how to include externally affected interests while remaining inside the empirical constraints set by current state borders. Arguably, state borders remain part of the 'circumstances of democracy', which are the 'normal conditions under which democracy is both empirically possible and normatively necessary' (Bauböck, 2017, p. 7). Citizenship and the capacity to express one's voice in a democracy depend on a (relatively) bounded demos. As Rainer Bauböck argues, 'consolidated territorial jurisdictions, which need not be united under a single sovereign authority, create conditions under which subjects have reasons for preferring voice over exit and rulers have reasons to be responsive to their subjects' (Bauböck, 2017, p. 14). Song (2012, pp. 59–60) also argues that 'the demos should be bounded by the state because the state secures the substantive conditions of democracy, serves as the primary site of solidarity conducive to democratic participation, and establishes clear links between representatives and their constituents'. Following this line of argument, a relatively bounded demos enhances the responsibility of its members for their decisions, the accountability of their representatives and the overall continuity of its institutions. I do not intend to defend the 'circumstances of democracy' as strictly normative conditions; rather, I consider them as a given premise in order to explore achievable forms of inclusion that are compatible with political borders as we know them. My question is, then, how can we articulate the due consideration of non-citizens whose interests are affected by migration policies while preserving a demos able to exercise self-determination?[1]

A vast literature has emerged in democratic theory on how to appropriately select and define a principle of legitimate inclusion. Disputes regarding its scope of application and whether such a principle disrupts democratic institutions, citizenship and territorial borders have complexified the initial 'boundary problem' considerably (Owen, 2012; Whelan, 1983). Instead of engaging directly with this normative literature, I wish to spell out one of its possible outcomes, i.e. inclusion as representation. I embrace a form of statist cosmopolitanism (Ypi, 2008) and look at the institutional translation of inclusion given the circumstances of democracy. I argue that representation within nation-states could be the locus of justificatory practices towards non-citizens and establish political institutions and practices that can realise the minimal inclusion of all externally affected individuals. Representation can satisfy both the cosmopolitan concern for the equal consideration of interests and the statist emphasis on the importance of having borders bound the demos territorially and civically. To demonstrate this claim, I will defend ad hoc implementations that make representation more inclusive. These implementations encompass electoral, non-electoral and surrogate representation as well as participatory and advocacy practices.

Briefly put, I examine the inclusive function of representation and develop the representational form of the All-Affected Principle (AAP) as a feasible first step to realising the principle. Hence, I will not consider the possibility of simply enfranchising people whose interests are affected.[2] I focus instead on the justification of representation as the institutional form of due consideration owed to people whose interests are affected. In Section 1, I justify why it is crucial to consider externally affected interests. I adopt the AAP and argue that it could be institutionalised through representation: individuals who are affected by a law or decision should, at a minimum, have their interests represented in the institutions deliberating and deciding about that law or decision. I then expand on my inclusive understanding of representation, encompassing advocacy or surrogate forms. In Section 2, I define the constructivist view of representation and interests on which I rely to further justify representation as an inclusion device. In Section 3, I assess different possible approaches to institutionalising the AAP through representation, namely reciprocal representation, self-appointed representatives, ombudspersons, advocacy groups and deliberative forums. In Section 4, I consider the functions these institutions perform and discuss the ad hoc political arrangements necessary to articulate the different representative practices in conjunction with each other and negotiate the claims made by a heterogeneous group like non-citizens.

Inclusion through representation

When global migratory movements involve more than 270 million people, the vision of a world made up of perfectly independent and autonomous states is no longer realistic. It is necessary to acknowledge the fact of migration. Current contentious issues like the attribution of political rights to foreign residents, the long-term settling of refugees or the legal precariousness of 'irregular' migrants highlight a multi-layered discrepancy between *de facto* participation and *de jure* inclusion. This lack of congruence creates a legitimacy gap: democratic norms of inclusion mandating that those who are subjected to or affected by laws should have some say in their creation clash with national practices of border governance. What is needed is better control of the effects of democratic decisions that reach beyond territorial and civic borders, i.e. laws and decisions that affect people who do not belong to the demos, whether they reside inside or outside its territory.

In order to make democratic values the guiding principles for nation-states' policies, one should take into consideration non-citizens whose interests are affected by these policies. The normative argument for democratic inclusion in the context of migration is based on the following premise: greater inclusion of non-citizens allows both (i.) a better realisation of democratic principles and (ii.) more control by non-citizens over the powers that affect their social and political life. (i.) Since democratic deliberation and decision-making procedures work better and more fairly when they include the different affected interests, representatives must include the affected interests of citizens and non-citizens in their deliberation procedures (input) and take them into consideration when assessing the application and consequences of these decisions (output). (ii.) And since the possibility for people to participate in decisions that impact them is central to the logic of the democratisation of power relations (Shapiro, 1999), it ought to be available to non-citizens. Otherwise, they remain subdued by what Michael Walzer famously termed the 'most common form of tyranny in human history,' 'the rule of citizens over non-citizens, of members over strangers' (Walzer, 1983, p. 62).

Three principles of democratic inclusion have been put forward: the All-Affected Principle (AAP), the All-Subjected Principle (ASP) and the Stakeholder Principle (SP). The AAP states that individuals whose interests are affected by a decision should be duly considered by being given a voice in the decision-making (Dahl, 1970, p. 49; Shapiro, 1999, p. 37; Young, 2000, pp. 5–6). The ASP posits that anyone coerced by a political authority should be the source of this authority. In other words, 'all and only those who are de facto subjected to coercive legal decisions should have a say in the making of those decisions' (Valentini, 2014, p. 792). Finally, according to the stakeholder principle, individuals whose 'autonomy and wellbeing is linked to the collective self-government and flourishing of a particular polity' (Bauböck, 2015, p. 824) should become or remain citizens of it.

As is commonly argued by its many critics, the AAP risks stretching the demos so far that it stops being a demos (Miller, 2009). Since it is possible to show that everyone can be potentially affected by any decision, in one way or another, the AAP inevitably has a cosmopolitan scope.[3] In fact, the same applies to the more intuitively limited ASP. Robert Goodin (2016) has forcefully argued that even the ASP leads to the enfranchisement of many people who remain far away from the polity while still being subjected to the polity's laws. Thus, the institutionalisation of such an inclusive concept remains contentious and could have detrimental effects upon democratic governance, shifting too far from the 'circumstances of democracy'.

I do not wish to engage in the conceptual debates regarding the exact articulation of these different principles. Rather, I focus on the AAP as a principle broadly requiring the consideration of externally affected interests and argue that representation is the basic mechanism for realising this principle: individuals who are affected by a law or decision should at a minimum have their interests represented in the institutions deliberating and deciding on that law or decision.

Many interpretations of the inclusion of externally affected interests have focused on enfranchisement: being considered and granted some voice over impactful decisions means having a right to vote (Angell & Huseby, 2017; Beckman, 2006; Ziegler, 2017). However, as I have begun to demonstrate, the practical consequences can be contentious. On the one hand, an unbounded or global demos might be the inevitable conclusion of democratic inclusion (Goodin, 2007; Valentini, 2014), which would jeopardise borders as we know them. On the other hand, there might still be a large number of people in need of consideration without a legitimate right to vote or whose right to vote needs to be supplemented by more active and diverse practices of interest representation. Non-citizens might indeed constitute a structural minority or remain socially excluded despite legal recognition. The sociological literature has clearly illustrated how non-citizens tend to participate less in the political life of the host country. Different factors, such as low socio-economic status, lack of familiarity with the political system, unequal access to informal channels of information, approximate knowledge of the official language, fear towards state bureaucracy, and so on, impede the disposition to vote (Hammar, 1994). Consequently, mere enfranchisement might give non-citizens votes without sufficient traction to impact elections and the interests of representatives.

In sum, enfranchisement alone might lead either to the unrealistic inclusion of all or enduring forms of exclusion. I suggest that representation encompasses the aspiration to expand consideration and offers practical channels of inclusion. Representation comprises different forms of electoral and non-electoral representation, advocacy and deliberative groups and surrogate representation, i.e. representatives speaking or acting for constituents who did not vote for them (Mansbridge, 2003). Realising the AAP via representation might be less inclusive than the enfranchisement of all, but this approach is still more inclusive than mere awareness (Kumm, 2016, p. 245). Hence, a representational interpretation of the AAP seems a necessary supplement to democracy to ensure that all affected interests are considered even when the interest bearers cannot (or should not) vote.

To further justify this point, I should address one immediate possible objection related to surrogate forms of representation for non-citizens as opposed to enfranchisement. Surrogate representation is usually defended for people who cannot be part of the constituency. Notably, surrogate representation is more meaningful than enfranchisement for people without clear agency or autonomy, such as children, future generations, or non-human animals. Is it acceptable, then, to imagine that non-citizens need non-elected representatives when they are human adults who can explicitly voice their interests and needs by themselves? I argue that the exclusion of non-citizens from surrogate representation solely because they are physically able to participate is illegitimate. Again, this exclusion is based on an abstract view of political agency, according to which people participate whenever technically able to do so. A framework that is sensitive to social barriers to participation informs the normative argument for representation of affected interests. Inclusion cannot be strictly legalistic; enfranchisement as the sole way of realising inclusion is not satisfying.

An institutional orientation to the AAP has already been defended (Benvenisti, 2013; Koenig-Archibugi, 2017; Montanaro, 2017; Ron, 2017), but its realisation through representation in the context of migration scarcely appears in the normative literature, where it is mentioned but not elaborated on (Bauböck, 2017, pp. 24–26; Goodin, 2016, p. 385; Landemore, 2020, pp. - 214–215; Miller, 2009, pp. 223–224). Overall, while the empirical literature has documented the many ways the interests of those legally or politically marginalised are effectively voiced in daily politics, a normative framework for the democratic representation of non-citizens' interests is still missing. Such a framework could reconcile democratic aspirations for inclusion and political channels of governance. This framework relies on the AAP but embeds the principle in the current constraints of bounded democracies.

The scope of representation for non-citizens is limited in two ways. First, the decision in question must be related to issues affecting non-citizens. Second, representation should not replace pre-existing paths to inclusion. Representing the interests of non-citizens should not preclude stronger forms of inclusion, such as citizenship rights for long-term foreign residents. Representation is the second-best option for people who would be included in the demos under a literal application of the AAP but who are not due to the functional constraints of democracies.

A constructivist account of representation and interests

Before developing more in-depth what representing externally affected interests could look like in practice, I need to make an epistemological point to justify my articulation of representation and affected interests.

Representation, classically understood, relies on the formation of relatively closed constituencies that are representable, whereas the AAP requires flexibility and the consideration of non-constituents. The 'standard account' of representation indeed '1) presupposes territorial constituencies with more or less rationally specifiable interests; 2) reduces political representation to parliamentary representation; 3) models it juridically as a principal-agent relationship; and 4) requires that relationship to be unidirectional with the representative taking the principal or constituency as its reference point' (Disch, 2015, p. 489). By contrast, the constructivist account of representation suggests that representation encompasses more flexible, informal and multifaceted practices. Its main tenet is 'to conceptualize representative and represented as linked not by a static "correspondence" but in a dynamic process of mutual constitution' (Disch, 2015, p. 489).[4] This constructivist account seems more suitable for including in the analysis the many shapes and sizes representation can take in practice and normatively more desirable as it expands the domain of democratic deliberation to representational practices previously considered apolitical, informal or marginal. Therefore, a constructivist understanding of representation is conceptually fruitful for my argument of representing the interests of people who are not part of the national constituency.

This approach, however, poses a conundrum: representation is understood in a constructivist manner, while the focus on interests suggests an objectivist and aggregative vision of politics. People have clear interests, which either need to be taken into account or not. Does that imply, then, that implementing the AAP through representation is incoherent? I suggest that a constructivist understanding of both representation and interests will help solve these tensions. I argue that interests should not be understood as already given, fixed and objective. They are relational and partially constructed through the very practice of representation.

Interests need not be defined in an objectivist way, referring to a pre-political moral consensus on what is generally desirable for human beings or to a universal human nature with biological non-contestable needs. Having one's interests affected is a process of becoming aware of certain relations of impact. To become aware of one's interests means shaping (rather than discovering) them politically in response to power relations. Thus, interests exist as the basis of claims and rights to ensure that their bearers participate in their definition in order to control what affects them. Interests are neither strictly subjective (as opposed to wants or desires) nor strictly objective (pre-politically given); they are *relational*. They are the grounds for people's objection to power, either because it affects them negatively (domination) or, when the affection is positive, because it excludes them from its exercise (paternalism). They are based on the intimate knowledge individuals have about those, and on the power structure in which they are enshrined. What matters is the relation between the affecting and the affected agent, i.e. to consider whether the affected agent have a say in the shaping of her interests, and some control over the affection.

The AAP helps track these power relations and buttresses claims to consideration and inclusion. In this way, the AAP constructs publics, which I interpret from a pragmatist perspective: 'The public consists of those who are affected by the indirect consequences of transactions to such an extent that it is deemed necessary to have those consequences systematically cared for' (Dewey, 1954, p. 16). This definition rests upon an equal capacity to be affected and a common interest in either not being affected or controlling this affection (i.e. controlling the scope of the externalities of power). This means that a public does not exist because of a pre-political identity, but coalesces through reactions to the negative consequences that affect it. What shapes a public is a common struggle against negative affection, i.e. domination or injustice, which the AAP helps diagnose (Dewey, 1954, pp. 16–17; Koenig-Archibugi, 2017, p. 184). A public arises from the reflexive control of what affects it.

This constructivist interpretation of interests should be understood in conjunction with the constructivist approach to representation I describe above. As Richard Bellamy and Dario Castiglione argue in the context of representation in the EU:

> Representatives neither appeal to the passive assent of the unreflective, naked preferences of citizens, nor merely reproduce their particular sectional interests, or the alleged prepolitical interests of a collective body. Rather, the incentives are such that they need to employ public reasons that can be avowed and shared by a broad cross- section of the citizenry. Such public reasoning leads citizens to reflect upon their interests in ways that help construct shared interests (Bellamy & Castiglione, 2013, p. 212).

The constructivist account of political representation departs from the conception of an already existing agent (e.g. an individual, the people, the working class) that representation makes present where or when absent (Pitkin, 1967, pp. 8–9). Representation is a practice happening when a would-be representative publicly makes a representative claim towards an agent who is then constituted as a would-be represented agent by this very claim (Saward, 2010). In a nutshell, representation is performative. The discourses and actions of claiming representation coalesce the interests, identity and unity of an agent. However, they do not construct them out of nothing. Building on my earlier point regarding the construction of interests, I am employing a *moderate* constructionism. I assume, paraphrasing Abbott (1995, p. 863), that any practice of representation 'begins with what is in part a soup of pre-existing actors and actions.' This metaphysical prudence does not preclude the constructivist characterisation of both the representative (e.g. as a 'good' representative) and the represented (e.g. as having specific interests). However, the extent to which these characterisations are based on already existing material is beyond my point. What matters is that the representatives, in speaking and acting for others, coalesce a public into being rather than directly constructing it and represent and shape its interests, self-image or political goals through their representative claim.

The performative approach to representation has at least two consequences. As a performance, representation may fail if, for instance, it is contested by the represented, and this contestation is unsuccessfully adjusted to by the representative. The relation between represented and representative is dynamic and involves power: the power of the claim maker to shape an agent and gain legitimacy by speaking in its name, and the power of the agent to contest or reject the claim or call for another kind of representation or other representatives. As Fossen (2019, p. 826) argues, 'a relation of representation is never a *fait accompli*, but at best a fragile achievement that remains subject to potential contestation'. Hence, representative claims participate actively in the construction, conscientization and publicisation of the interests of the represented and allow for the participation of the represented to exercise their political agency to debate, negotiate, reject or accept the claims made in their name (Montanaro, 2017, p. 210). Representation is *democratic* precisely when the represented '*gain* ... some agency in the process, otherwise representative democracy would only be a "second best" or a "defective substitute" for direct democracy' (Hayat, 2019, p. 131).

The second implication of a constructivist approach to representation is that representation becomes more multifaceted. It describes more generally 'the activities of actors like civil society advocates, stakeholders, spokespeople, media commentators and a host of other "representers" in a wide variety of political contexts,' based on the premise that 'there can be no legitimate authority without channels for popular representation,' argues Daniel Bray (2011, p. 39). As I will explore in the next section, considering representation as a performative claim reveals many more instances of representation besides the dyadic perception of electoral representation between a constituency and its representative.

These features of a constructivist conception of interests and representation are particularly relevant when the 'constituency' or 'audience' of the representative claim has no right to vote. Representing the interests of non-citizens can happen below or beyond electoral forms of political representation. When the represented are excluded, contesting representative claims poses specific challenges to exercising agency. If someone starts speaking in the name of the 'undocumented', it may become more difficult for actual undocumented immigrants to voice their opposition and suggest counterclaims as such actions might aggravate their precarious socio-legal situation.

Hence, the usefulness of the broader concept of 'inclusive representation', defined by Hayat (2019, p. 136) as 'any form of representative claim or system of representative claims that has as its consequence the increase of direct participation and the proliferation of activities of testing claims by the represented.' Individuals whose interests are affected constitute 'moral constituents' (Thompson, 1999, p. 120) whom, I argue, surrogate representatives ought to be accountable for. The process of representing externally affected interests is more open than typical electoral forms and more diverse than dyadic forms (between voters and representatives). It includes non-elective and collective forms of representation as well as advocacy and surrogate representation.

Inclusive representation in practice

I have made a case for the representation of the affected interests of non-citizens; in this section, I detail possible approaches to implementing such representation. However, I first want to consider whether such a case is at all necessary considering current institutions. Elizabeth Cohen has argued that 'non-citizen interests in fact do receive representation':

> Their interests are not only being protected because businesses stand to profit or because they have family members in this country, both of which would constitute an indirect form of trusteeship. Governors, senators, and even the President have also spoken on behalf of the interests of the undocumented. (Cohen, 2014, p. 1065)

I agree with Cohen that representatives act as surrogate representatives when they advocate for the interests of people who did not vote for them, who did not vote at all or who do not belong to the demos. This surrogate representation does not mean, however, that all interests – for instance, those pertaining to concrete experiences of denizenship and exclusion for undocumented migrants or the illegitimate exclusion happening at or beyond the demos' borders – are *adequately* represented. The fact that some non-citizens' interests are intertwined with those of citizens and are therefore represented does not undermine the validity of institutionalising more inclusive forms of representation. Indeed, the fact that some forms of inclusive representation are already at work further demonstrate that such representation is feasible and needs to be systematically justified and empirically intensified.

The question then arises as to which institutional forms the representation of externally affected interests can take. Following my previous point, it is possible to first distinguish between practices that pool the interests of citizens and non-citizens and practices that focus exclusively on non-citizens. A second distinction concerns whether the representation takes place within or outside an already-established parliamentary system. Indeed, implementations of inclusive representation can act as a spur to deliberating new claims, encouraging contestation through representative 'advocacy agencies or channels of dissent' (Kuper, 2004, p. 107) that do not necessarily exist within parliaments. I will assess the following options:

	Representing the interests of citizens and non-citizens together	Representing the interests of non-citizens only
Parliamentary	Supranational parliament	Reciprocal representation
Non-parliamentary	Ombudsperson	Self-appointed representatives, advocacy groups

These proposals might already exist independently, but when taken together as a collection, they present a systemic approach to realising the AAP for non-citizens and supplementing existing forms of representation. Taken separately, each offers limited forms of inclusion or might fall short of the ideal of a fully transnational representative democracy; taken together, they constitute repertoires of representational inclusion.

A supranational parliament provides a framework – beyond borders – to foster democratic accountability, consideration of affected foreign interests, equal sharing of power and equal deliberation. Such representation happening beyond the state yet based on a statist structure captures the dual commitment to the consideration of externally affected interests and the circumstances of democracy (Lord, 2019). The European Parliament is the working example of supranational shared sovereignty, law-making power, deliberation and decision-making procedures. Such institutions embody the ideal of *demoi*-cracy, guaranteeing the justification of impactful decisions, the equal consideration of interests and the equal status of concerned parties (Bellamy & Castiglione, 2019; Lord, 2013).

Reciprocal representation is a more embryonic form of transnational parliamentary representation focusing solely on the representation of non-citizens. As advocated by Philippe Schmitter, it would consist for states between which migratory movements happen in 'accord[ing] each other seats in their respective national legislatures. The number of seats – perhaps two or three – could vary, depending on mutual perceptions of the degree of interdependence, as well as the total number of deputies in each legislature' (Schmitter, 1997, p. 303). The nomination of one or several non-citizens' representatives in national legislatures could strongly foster non-citizens' interests. Joachim Blatter has recently revived this proposal at the European scale, calling for 'transnationalising national elections, parties and parliaments' through a 'consociation of nation states' that 'grants the consociated citizens the right to elect a limited number of special representations in its national parliament' (Blatter, 2019). Jeremy Bentham had already suggested a similar proposal to exchange members of parliament entrusted with agenda-setting competence. Granting a few seats to foreigners in national legislatures would have diplomatic and epistemic benefits through the building of mutual trust between nations as a guarantor of peace and by bringing new and impartial perspectives into parliament (Niesen, 2019). Frazer (2014) also argues for the impartiality of foreign members in solving ad hoc internal disputes or monitoring national representation. This kind of epistemic benefit also concerns citizens: reciprocal representation enhances citizens' awareness of transnational issues and of the special responsibilities their country shares with others (Lacey, 2019).

An often-cited institution for including non-voting members and non-members (e.g. foreigners but also children or future generations) is the ombudsperson. The recent example of the French '*défenseur des droits*' (rights defender) is instructive (Rivière, 2020). While in office between 2014 and 2020, Jacques Toubon was particularly active, publicising various cases involving the violation of fundamental rights of migrants in parliament hearings and the media. Toubon made public statements in favour of letting the humanitarian boat *Aquarius* dock in France; testified against the contested bone examination of minor migrants to determine their age, deeming it ineffective and inhumane; and regularly alerted public authorities to the living conditions of migrants in unauthorised camps, calling on the government to protect the most vulnerable inhabitants. These types of interventions, shared by many non-governmental and local organisations, gain public, legal and political tractions when made by an authorised ombuds institution.

Non-parliamentary forms of representation of non-citizen interests might constitute necessary supplements to parliamentary options. 'Inclusive representation' is conceptualised precisely to encompass more participatory politics. As Hayat argues:

> Inclusive representation is realized through the participation of the represented in the discussion of collective outcomes and of representative claims, but also in the pluralization of these claims. Indeed, some forms of inclusion can be internal to the existing means of representation (politicization, judgment on elected representatives), or external to them, through the formation of alternate representative claims, in social movements [. . .], NGOs, and so on, in order to equip the represented with other means of recognition and action. (Hayat, 2019, p. 136)

A flexible mode of representation of individuals whose interests are affected by foreign decisions rely on self-appointed representatives. As Laura Montanaro describes them: 'they make claims to represent others outside of electoral institutions or offices and apart from state authority ... [They] may play an important role in democracy, particularly in a complex and globalizing world, where electoral constituencies fail to coincide with those affected by collective decisions' (Montanaro, 2012, p. 1094). Decoupling representation from democratic territoriality and gradually voicing the interests of individuals excluded from normal parliamentary representation is a compelling way of institutionalising the AAP. While the institutional power and visibility of self-appointed representatives may be limited to the very moment they make a claim, their capacity to create transnational publics (raising awareness of the interests of the affected people in question) and influence agenda-setting and public opinion gives them significant political clout.[5]

Self-appointed representatives can organise further in advocacy and deliberative groups such as lobbies, committees, commissions, transnational meetings and NGOs. Furthermore, they can defend the interests of non-citizens by reviewing policy proposals and advocating for the consideration of non-citizens in national and international political agendas. Several theoretical proposals for such representative initiatives either within or between states have already been made: a 'chamber of discourses' (Dryzek & Niemeyer, 2008), a 'tribune for non-citizens' (Thompson, 1999, pp. 121–122), transnational courts assessing externalities and claims of affected interests (Held, 1995, p. 237) and a global parliament or 'People's Assembly' (Archibugi et al., 2000). In practice, taking the situation in Europe as an example, the Migrant's Forum (now the European Migration Forum), the European Council on Refugees and Exiles and coalitions such as the Starting Line Group are evidence of the possibility of gathering representatives (e.g. NGOs, activists, lobbyists, etc.) to influence migration-related international agendas. Further, institutional metaphors can help reclaim official political labels to legitimize activist advocacy groups. We can think of the Permanent Peoples' Tribunal and its 'sentence' pronounced in January 2018 against the 'violations of the rights of migrants and refugees;'[6] the Universal Embassy which occupied the former Somali embassy building in Brussels from 2000 to 2005 to defend undocumented migrants[7]; the Refugee and Migrant Parliament which gathered pro-migrant organisations at the European Parliament in 2018[8]; or even artistic productions such as the fresco *Embassy of the Refugee* by Caleb Duarte and Mari Martinez in Oakland (Schreiber, 2021). This last example points to the importance of artistic productions as advocacy. Art participates in the construction of affected publics. Pictorial, musical or theatrical performances are means of mobilisation, participation, identity formation, diffusion of narratives and depictions of migrant life or public awareness campaigns that constitute the broad view of inclusive representation I am arguing for (Blomfield & Lenette, 2018; Martiniello, 2019). An ethics of representation – i.e. how one accurately characterises what or who is represented and the intentions behind and effects of such a characterisation – is inherent to political representation (Sager, 2019).

Ad hoc arrangements: the politics of inclusive representation

In the following section, I discuss the limits of these representative institutions and practices to delineate the political dimension of inclusive representation and the ad hoc arrangements it might require.

Viewed separately, each practice has weaknesses. In the European Union, the large scale of a transnational parliament does not by itself solve the lack of representation of non-citizens. Affected non-European interests are still neglected, and the various criticisms of undemocratic governance (also echoed regarding United Nations institutions) tarnish the Union's accomplishments. As reciprocal representation works on a bilateral basis, it remains highly selective in its interest consideration and merely ratifies pre-existing political ties occurring through usual diplomatic channels. An ombudsperson is a top-down form of rights protection that might be too dependent on the executive power and hence too politicised and remote from local demands. Furthermore, as Sofia Näsström (2019) wrote, these institutional innovations could rightfully be seen as 'a democratic decoy, a step towards more technocracy rather than more democracy'. Advocacy groups and self-appointed representatives raise challenging issues related to accountability, the democratic legitimacy of individuals speaking in the name of others and the personalisation of collective and complex causes. More generally, advocacy and deliberative activities might simply lack political leverage. However, this eventual weakness is a part of my point. Devising ways to institutionalise the AAP through representation aims at empowering inclusion, i.e. going further than mere consultation. I am arguing for representation as a first step, which may need supplementing with more concrete forms of participatory politics, such as local voting, unionisation, demonstrations, civil disobedience and so forth.[9]

In fact, these possible forms of representation operate at different levels, from transnational parliamentary bodies to local artistic practices, and allow claims of different intensities. They complement each other through ad hoc arrangements. Inclusive representation encompasses a collection of representative practices and forums and, as Kuyper (2016, pp. 308–309) argues, they 'can be internally undemocratic, or act in non-deliberative ways, yet still fulfil democratic functions within the broader system.'

Following Mark Warren's systemic approach to democratic functioning, representation fills three different functions: 'empowered inclusion' ('expands inclusion over time and space'), 'collective agenda and will formation' ('enables perspective-taking, enables small-group deliberation'), and 'collective-decision-making' ('representative bodies can function as accountable decision-making bodies'; Warren, 2017, p. 46; Kuyper, 2016). The different practices and institutions I have assessed are coherent with this functionalist perspective, the first two functions being filled by non-parliamentary representation, the third one by parliamentary representation. They also expand the perspective by taking the specific interests of non-citizens into consideration or by giving equal consideration to the interests of citizens and non-citizens. While artistic productions can appear anywhere – an artist making a statement in the name of migrants, for instance, – they can grow into more institutionalised claims when they raise civil and political awareness. Self-appointed representatives can move from local activism to national representation, climbing the political ladder through their demands for better inclusion. Reciprocal representation between countries sharing a migration agenda can entrench compacts or large decisions made at the transnational parliamentary level.

There is often a suspicion that non-electoral representation lacks authorisation and accountability (Chandler, 2012, pp. 106–107), which might lead to more formal awareness. For the representative, not risking any electoral sanctions or rewards from a non-voting constituency might trivialise and marginalise the represented interests. John Stuart Mill (1977, p. 470) put it well:

> Rulers and ruling classes are under a necessity of considering the interests and wishes of those who have the suffrage; but of those who are excluded, it is in their option whether they will do so or not; and however honestly disposed, they are in general too fully occupied with things which they must attend to, to have much room in their thoughts for anything which they can with impunity disregard.

However, inclusive representation aims precisely at replacing this dyadic view of accountability and representation with a collective one. Practices of virtual, collective or surrogate representation already occur in classically defined nation-states since representatives also represent the minority of people who did not vote for them (Weissberg, 1978, p. 537; Mansbridge, 2003, pp. 522–524). In those cases, accountability can be detached from representation. The representative does not respond directly to their moral or virtual constituency, but that does not prevent accountability assessments through independent 'channels of scrutiny' and 'monitoring bodies' (Maia, 2012, p. 432). The role of journalists or migrants' advocates can involve close examination of the quality (i.e. legitimacy and efficacy) of the claim to representation.

Inclusive representation also runs the risk of appropriating rather than making audible the voices of others. Any instances of speaking for or in the name of others should always be scrutinised (Spivak, 1990, p. 64). It is the usual bargaining nature of political action to devise ways to balance the questions of who will most accurately represent a group's interests and who will have the highest likelihood of dismantling the domination that excludes that group. Descriptive representation may partially alleviate the kind of paternalism Spivak discusses: migrants may demand to be represented by migrants. As Mansbridge (1999) has shown, descriptive representation has positive effects such as improving the epistemic quality of deliberation, and hence the legitimacy of decisions; easing communication and trust between representatives and represented; and giving marginalised groups a sense of being able to rule.

Proponents of group representation have also pointed to the dilemma of the necessity and the impossibility of representing minority groups without essentialising and altering the group itself (Phillips, 1998; Young, 2000). Phillips (1998, p. 188) suggested introducing 'mechanisms of accountability' within groups, which provide internal deliberative processes for autonomous groups but are unlikely to work for a group as diverse as non-citizens. Young's approach may be more useful, arguing that a group does not have to be defined through a collective identity. Individuals form groups when they share *perspectives*. A perspective is 'a way of looking at social processes without determining what one sees. . . . Sharing a perspective . . . gives each an affinity with the other's way of describing what he experiences, an affinity that those differently situated do not experience' (Young, 2000, p. 137). While migrants occupy different social positions, they might share perspectives on certain problems (e.g. access to public services, freedom of movement, discrimination, etc.). They form a shared interest in being represented in order to voice an experience unknown to non-migrants. If women or racialised individuals can act as – or legitimately claim to be represented as – a group, non-citizens can too; they are not inherently more diverse. Politically speaking, the pooling of perspectives and interests can rely on 'a *strategic* use of positivist essentialism in a scrupulously visible political interest' (Spivak, 1988, p. 205). In other words, while non-citizens groups surely possess conflicting interests and values, they might band together, based on their common status or social position, for the sake of political gain. Essentialism legitimises the commonality and authenticity of their claim; strategy prevents long-term ascription to the group.

On a more practical level, this dilemma has been the main problem for the European Migrants' Forum in the 1990s. As Guiraudon (2001) explains, 'all studies of the Migrants' Forum point out numerous difficulties in finding common ground among the migrant lobby groups and in defining an agenda. . . . The Migrants' Forum was very divided, as different ethnic groups publicly expressed antagonism'. However, the quandary does not invalidate the need for inclusive representation but instead points to the conflicts which can result from institutionalising inclusive representation. Only a naïve understanding of collective action, interests and democracy, in general, would discard a principle solely because power-laden practices make it difficult to realise.

In sum, the representation of non-citizens plays a vital democratic role and serves different functions not limited to elective practices, such as including externally affected perspectives and interests in deliberating and decision-making bodies; crystalising interests to build common political claims; informing the general public about the conditions of vulnerable migrants due to their legal status (or absence thereof); regaining control of images and narratives from populist misrepresentation; and advocating the cause of migration policy reform. While, in most cases, some form of imperfect representation is a necessary but insufficient step towards future inclusion, combining imperfect forms of representation (and accumulating them over time) might gradually adjust the ideal of inclusion and the practices of nation-states.

Conclusion

I have argued for the representation of non-citizens as a practical form of due consideration of their interests and a second-best alternative to their inclusion in the demos. Starting from the intuitively moral principle underpinning the AAP but remaining constrained by realist premises of democratic functioning, electoral and non-electoral forms of representation of non-citizens' affected interests could solve the tension between this norm of inclusion and a bounded demos. If the existence of both borders and externalities impacting non-citizens is inevitable, representation offers a desirable method for including their interests in deliberative, agenda-setting and decision-making processes through parliamentary and non-parliamentary mechanisms.

The different forms of inclusive representation each have associated problems, but – taken together as performing different functions – they realise the due consideration owed to non-citizens and give weight to non-citizens' claims. The AAP and its institutionalisation through representation suggest an alternative route to the all-or-nothing defence of inclusion, which suggests the radical enfranchisement of people affected beyond borders. Inclusive representation offers more modest but feasible avenues of providing non-citizens with wider moral consideration, formal inclusion in deliberation, and even a voice in decision-making procedures while acknowledging the realist circumstances of democracy.

Notes

1. This is a timely challenge, especially for countries that need to both respond to ongoing demands from public opinions for stronger border controls and justify their policies according to liberal and democratic norms. On this tension see, Hidalgo (2019).
2. Such enfranchisement would be justified by stronger principles of inclusion, such as the All-Subjected Principle (ASP) or the Stakeholder Principle (SP), which I will briefly discuss later. Fundamentally, these principles require a right to vote for all those subject to laws and decisions, usually legitimating local and transnational voting rights for foreign residents (Arrighi & Bauböck, 2017).
3. This most extensive 'possibilist' interpretation of the AAP (Goodin, 2007) is one among several. See, Hultin Rosenberg (2020) for a reappraisal of the problem and the reformulation of the AAP as 'the principle that requires inclusion in the demos of all those and only those who are better or worse off as a foreseeable consequence of a decision that the state is in a position to take' (Hultin Rosenberg, 2020, p. 866).
4. On this 'constructivist turn', see, Brito Vieira (2017), Castiglione and Pollak (2018), and Disch et al. (2019),
5. See also, Knops and Severs (2019) for a case applied to refugees. See, Rubenstein (2014) to justify further the need to control the claim made by self-appointed representatives and advocates.

6. See http://permanentpeoplestribunal.org/session-on-the-violation-of-human-rights-of-migrants-and-refugee-people-the-verdicts-of-palermo-and-paris/?lang=en (accessed 16 April 2019).
7. See the statement online http://www.ieb.be/IMG/pdf/declaration-de-l-ambassade-universelle_12-12-2001.pdf (accessed 16 April 2019).
8. See the resolution it adopted: http://www.migrantwomennetwork.org/wp-content/uploads/2019/01/FINAL-RESOLUTION-18-Oct-2018-Refugee-Migrant-Parliament.pdf (accessed 5 May 2020).
9. I am not arguing that participation should be mandatory to be allowed a claim to inclusion or representation, but that inclusion necessitates access to channels of expression other than representation. Deciding to not get involved, to opt out, should always remain an option that does not detrimentally impact claims to protection, legal standing and moral and political consideration.

Acknowledgments

This work was supported by the Max Planck Institute for the Study of Religious and Ethnic Diversity. I am grateful to the director of the department of Ethics, Law and Politics, Ayelet Shachar, for her trust in organizing the workshop "Inclusive Parliaments: Representation, Mobility, Disability" and pursuing with this special issue. For comments on an earlier versions of this paper, presented at the Max Planck Institute, the ECPR General Conference, and the University of Hamburg, I wish to thank Svenja Ahlhaus, Ali Emre Benli, Tendayi Bloom, Marcus Carlsen Häggrot, Ran Hirschl, Simon Laumann Jørgensen, Peter Niesen, Dominic Roser, Regina Schidel, and Marta Wojciechowska.

Disclosure statement

No potential conflict of interest was reported by the author(s).

ORCID

Benjamin Boudou http://orcid.org/0000-0003-2309-7303

References

Abbott, A. (1995). Things of boundaries. *Social Research*, *62*(4), 857–882. https://www.jstor.org/stable/40971127

Abizadeh, A. (2008). Democratic theory and border Coercion: No right to unilaterally control your own borders. *Political Theory*, *36*(1), 37–65. https://doi.org/10.1177/0090591707310090

Angell, K., & Huseby, R. (2017). Should irregular immigrants be (Rapidly) enfranchised? *Political Research Quarterly*, *70*(2), 363–373. https://doi.org/10.1177/1065912917695188

Archibugi, D., Balduini, S., & Donati, M. (2000). The United Nations as an agency of global democracy. In B. Holden (Ed.), *Global democracy: Key debates* (pp. 125–143). Routledge.

Arrighi, J.-T., & Bauböck, R. (2017). A multilevel puzzle: Migrants' voting rights in national and local elections. *European Journal of Political Research*, *56*(3), 619–639. https://doi.org/10.1111/1475-6765.12176

Bauböck, R. (2015). Morphing the demos into the right shape: Normative principles for enfranchising resident aliens and expatriate citizens. *Democratization*, *22*(5), 820–839. https://doi.org/10.1080/13510347.2014.988146

Bauböck, R. (2017). *Democratic inclusion: Rainer Bauböck in dialogue*. Manchester University Press.

Beckman, L. (2006). Citizenship and voting rights: Should resident aliens vote? *Citizenship Studies*, *10*(2), 153–165. https://doi.org/10.1080/13621020600633093

Bellamy, R., & Castiglione, D. (2013). Three models of democracy, political community and representation in the EU. *Journal of European Public Policy*, *20*(2), 206–223. https://doi.org/10.1080/13501763.2013.746118

Bellamy, R., & Castiglione, D. (2019). *From Maastricht to Brexit: Democracy, Constitutionalism and Citizenship in the EU*. Rowman and Littlefield.

Benvenisti, E. (2013). Sovereigns as trustees of humanity: On the accountability of states to foreign stakeholders. *The American Journal of International Law*, *107*(2), 295–333. https://doi.org/10.5305/amerjintelaw.107.2.0295

Blatter, J. (2019). Let me vote in your country, and I'll let you vote in mine: A proposal for transnational democracy. In J. Blatter & R. Bauböck Eds., *Let me vote in your country, and I'll let you vote in mine* EUI, Global Governance Programme. https://globalcit.eu/let-me-vote-in-your-country-and-ill-let-you-vote-in-mine-a-proposal-for-transnational-democracy

Blomfield, I., & Lenette, C. (2018). Artistic representations of refugees: What is the role of the artist? *Journal of Intercultural Studies*, *39*(3), 322–338. https://doi.org/10.1080/07256868.2018.1459517

Bray, D. (2011). *Pragmatic cosmopolitanism: Representation and leadership in transnational democracy*. Palgrave Macmillan .

Brito Vieira, M. (Ed.). (2017). *Reclaiming representation: contemporary advances in the theory of political representation*. Routledge.

Castiglione, D., & Pollak, J. (Eds.). (2018). *Creating political presence: The new politics of democratic representation*. The University of Chicago Press.

Chandler, D. (2012). The limits of post-territorial political community. In L. Beckman & E. Erman (Eds.), *Territories of citizenship* (pp. 100–122). Palgrave Macmillan.

Cohen, E. (2014). Dilemmas of representation, citizenship, and semi-citizenship. *St. Louis University Law Journal*, *58*(4), 1047–1070. https://scholarship.law.slu.edu/lj/vol58/iss4/

Dahl, R. (1970). *After the revolution? Authority in a good society*. Yale University Press.
Dewey, J. (1954). *The public and its problems: An essay in political inquiry*. Swallow Press.
Disch, L. (2015). The 'constructivist turn' in democratic representation: A normative dead-end? *Constellations*, *22*(4), 487–499. https://doi.org/10.1111/1467-8675.12201
Disch, L., van de Sande, M., & Urbinati, N. (Eds.). (2019). *The constructivist turn in political representation*. Edinburgh University Press.
Dryzek, J., & Niemeyer, S. (2008). Discursive representation. *American Political Science Review*, *102*(4), 481–493. https://doi.org/10.1017/S0003055408080325
Fossen, T. (2019). Constructivism and the logic of political representation. *American Political Science Review*, *113*(3), 824–837. https://doi.org/10.1017/S0003055419000273
Frazer, M. (2014). Including the Unaffected. *The Journal of Philosophy*, *22*(4), 377–395. https://doi.org/10.1111/jopp.12024
Goodin, R. (2007). Enfranchising all affected interests, and its alternatives. *Philosophy and Public Affairs*, *35*(1), 40–68. https://doi.org/10.1111/j.1088-4963.2007.00098.x
Goodin, R. (2016). Enfranchising all subjected, worldwide. *International Theory*, *8*(3), 365–389. https://doi.org/10.1017/S1752971916000105
Guiraudon, V. (2001). Weak weapons of the weak? Transnational mobilization around migration in the European Union. In D. Imig & S. Tarrow (Eds.), *Contentious Europeans: Protest and politics in an emerging polity* (pp. 163–186). Rowman and Littlefield.
Hammar, T. (1994). *Democracy and the Nation State: Aliens, denizens and citizens in a world international migration*. Ashgate.
Hayat, S. (2019). Representation as proposition: Democratic representation after the constructivist turn. In L. Disch, M. V. D. Sande, & N. Urbinati (Eds.), *The constructivist turn in political representation* (pp. 121–140). Edinburgh University Press.
Held, D. (1995). *Democracy and the global order. From the modern state to cosmopolitan governance*. Polity Press.
Hidalgo, J. (2019). *Unjust borders: Individuals and the ethics of immigration*. Taylor & Francis.
Hultin Rosenberg, J. (2020). The all-affected principle reconsidered. *Social Theory and Practice*, *46*(4), 847–867. https://doi.org/10.5840/soctheorpract2020112107
Knops, L., & Severs, E. (2019). Self-appointed representatives on Facebook:The case of the Belgian Citizen's platform for refugee support. *International Journal of Communication*, *13*, 5610–5628. https://ijoc.org/index.php/ijoc/article/view/10806
Koenig-Archibugi, M. (2017). How to diagnose democratic deficits in global politics: The use of the 'all-affected principle. *International Theory*, *9*(2), 171–202. https://doi.org/10.1017/S1752971916000312
Kumm, M. (2016). Sovereignty and the right to be left alone: Subsidiarity, justice-sensitive externalities, and the proper domain of the consent requirement in international law. *Law and Contemporary Problems*, *79*(2), 239–258. https://scholarship.law.duke.edu/lcp/vol79/iss2/11
Kuper, A. (2004). *Democracy beyond borders: Justice and representation in global institutions*. Oxford University Press.
Kuyper, J. (2016). Systemic representation: democracy, deliberation, and nonelectoral representatives. *American Political Science Review*, *110*(2), 308–324. https://doi.org/10.1017/S0003055416000095

Lacey, J. (2019). Transnationally affected interests and multilateral decision-making: The limits of our institutional toolkit In J. Blatter & R. Bauböck (Eds.), *Let me vote in your country, and I'll let you vote in mine*. EUI, Global Governance Programme, GLOBALCIT.

Landemore, H. (2020). *Open democracy: Reinventing popular rule for the 20th Century*. Princeton University Press.

Lord, C. (2013). No representation without justification? Appraising standards of justification in European Parliament debates. *Journal of European Public Policy, 20* (2), 243–259. https://doi.org/10.1080/13501763.2013.746123

Lord, C. (2019). Externalities and representation beyond the state: Lessons from the European Union. In D. Castiglione & J. Pollak (Eds.), *Creating political presence: The new politics of democratic representation* (pp. 254–275). The University of Chicago Press.

Maia, R. C. M. (2012). Non-electoral political representation: Expanding discursive domains. *Representation, 48*(4), 429–443. https://doi.org/10.1080/00344893.2012.712547

Mansbridge, J. (1999). Should blacks represent blacks and women represent women? A contingent 'Yes'. *The Journal of Politics, 61*(3), 628–657. https://doi.org/10.2307/2647821

Mansbridge, J. (2003). Rethinking Representation. *The American Political Science Review, 97*(4), 515–528. https://doi.org/10.1017/S0003055403000856

Martiniello, M. (2019). Immigrants, refugees and the arts: A complex multidimensional relationship. In B. Dogramaci & M. Mersmann (Eds.), *Handbook of art and global migration: Theories, practices, and challenges* (pp. 70–75). De Gruyter.

Mill, J. S. (1977). Considerations on Representative government. In J. M. Robson (Ed.), *Collected works* (Vol. XIX). University of Toronto Press. 371–577 .

Miller, D. (2009). Democracy's domain. *Philosophy and Public Affairs, 37*(3), 201–228. https://doi.org/10.1111/j.1088-4963.2009.01158.x

Montanaro, L. (2012). The democratic legitimacy of self-appointed representatives. *The Journal of Politics, 74*(4), 1094–1107. https://doi.org/10.1017/S0022381612000515

Montanaro, L. (2017). Representing Affected Interests. In M. B. Vieira (Ed.), *Reclaiming representation: contemporary advances in the theory of political representation* (pp. 210–226). Routledge.

Näsström, S. (2019). Too little, too late. In J. Blatter & R. Bauböck (Eds.), *Let me vote in your country, and I'll let you vote in mine, EUI, global governance programme, GLOBALCIT.*

Niesen, P. (2019). Re-inventing the wheel? Reciprocal representation in bentham and blatter. In J. Blatter & R. Bauböck (Eds.), *Let me vote in your country, and I'll let you vote in mine, EUI, global governance programme, GLOBALCIT.*

Owen, D. (2012). Constituting the polity, constituting the demos: On the place of the all affected interests principle in democratic theory and in resolving the democratic boundary problem. *Ethics & Global Politics, 5*(3), 129–152. https://doi.org/10.3402/egp.v5i3.18617

Phillips, A. (1998). *The politics of presence*. Clarendon Press.

Pitkin, H. (1967). *The concept of representation*. 1967. University of California Press.

Rivière, C. (2020). La contribution du Défenseur des droits au respect effectif des droits des étrangers. *Les cahiers du Conseil constitutionnel, 6*. https://www.conseil-constitutionnel.fr/publications/titre-vii/la-contribution-du-defenseur-des-droits- au-respect-effectif-des-droits-des-etrangers

Ron, A. (2017). Affected interests and their institutions. *Democratic Theory*, *4*(2), 66–81. https://doi.org/10.3167/dt.2017.040205
Rubenstein, J. (2014). The misuse of power, not bad representation: Why it is beside the point that no one elected Oxfam. *Journal of Political Philosophy*, *22*(2), 204–230. https://doi.org/10.1111/jopp.12020
Rudiger, A., & Spencer, S. (2003). Social integration of migrants and ethnic minorities: Politics to combat discrimination. In: *The economic and social aspects of migration, Conference jointly organised by the European Commission and the OECD*, 21-22 January.
Sager, A. (2019). Ethics and migration crises. In C. Menjívar, M. Ruiz, & I. Ness (Eds.), *The Oxford handbook of migration crises* (pp. 589–602). Oxford University Press.
Saward, M. (2010). *The representative claim*. Oxford University Press.
Schmitter, P. (1997). Exploring the problematic triumph of liberal democracy and concluding with a modest proposal for improving its international impact. In A. Hadenius (Ed.), *Democracy's victory and crisis* (pp. 297–308). Cambridge University Press.
Schreiber, R. (2021). Performing sanctuary. *Migration and Society*, *4*(1), 76–83. https://doi.org/10.3167/arms.2021.040108
Shapiro, I. (1999). *Democratic justice*. Yale University Press.
song, S. (2012). The boundary problem in democratic theory: Why the demos should be bounded by the state. *International Theory*, *4*(1), 39–68. https://doi.org/10.1017/S1752971911000248
Spivak, G. (1988). *In other worlds: Essays in cultural politics*. Routledge.
Spivak, G. (1990). *The postcolonial critic: Interviews, strategies, dialogues*. Routledge.
Thompson, D. (1999). Democratic theory and global society. *The Journal of Political Philosophy*, *7*(2), 111–125. https://doi.org/10.1111/1467-9760.00069
Valentini, L. (2014). No global demos, no global democracy? A systematization and critique. *American Political Science Association*, *12*(4), 789–807. https://doi.org/10.1017/S1537592714002138
Walzer, M. (1983). *Spheres of justice: A defense of pluralism and equality*. Basic Books.
Warren, M. (2017). A problem-based approach to democratic theory. *American Political Science Review*, *111*(1), 39–53. https://doi.org/10.1017/S0003055416000605
Weissberg, R. (1978). Collective vs. dyadic representation in congress. *The American Political Science Review*, *72*(2), 535–547. https://doi.org/10.2307/1954109
Whelan, F. (1983). Democratic theory and the boundary problem. In R. Pennock & J. Chapman Eds., *Liberal Democracy. Nomos vol. 25* (13–47). New York University Press.
Young, I. (2000). *Inclusion and Democracy*. Oxford University Press.
Ypi, L. (2008). Statist cosmopolitanism. *The Journal of Political Philosophy*, *16*(1), 48–71. https://doi.org/10.1111/j.1467-9760.2008.00308.x
Ziegler, R. (2017). *Voting rights of refugees*. Cambridge University Press.

Index

Note: Page numbers followed by "n" denote endnotes.